MOTEL PLANNING AND BUSINESS MANAGEMENT

MOTEL PLANNING

Clare A. Gunn

AND BUSINESS MANAGEMENT

and   Robert W. McIntosh

Extension Specialists
School of Hotel, Restaurant and Institutional Management

Michigan State University
Eppley Center
East Lansing, Michigan

WM. C. BROWN COMPANY PUBLISHERS
Dubuque, Iowa

Preface

To many, the ownership of a motel is the pot of gold at the end of a dream rainbow. To others, it represents a potential quick return on a dollar invested. To some, motel management still appears simple and offers part-time or retirement job opportunity. The literature of the day contains little to prove the truth or fallacy of these popular opinions. Some specialized aspects of moteldom have been treated with thoroughness, but these are not generally available to the motel entrepreneur or student.

This text is offered as some help for those students, would-be owners, and hopeful managers who seek a simplified, theoretically sound, yet practical guide. It is a book about motels and motel management, no matter how defined, and as a compilation of information, it does not presume to substitute for experience. For the inexperienced, however, the ideas, facts, and practices here presented should help to hurdle several years of hard-knock experience. Even the experienced may find new approaches to expansion or remodeling problems.

The book is published at a time of sharpened motel competition. The motel building boom has passed its peak and the new motel, in order to survive, must be far superior to its progenitors in all respects. It must be better planned, better organized and better managed than ever before. The travel market continues to grow but is now more demanding, more selective, and more concerned over value received than in the past.

This endorses the need for forthright and up-to-date information on motelism.

This book has grown out of many years of close association with motel properties, facilities, and personnel during personal consultation and adult educational work. As hundreds of thousands of miles were traveled and thousands of establishments were visited, clues to success or failure were observed. From this vast pool of practical experience many conclusions have been drawn. But this alone might be misleading if not supported by the undergirding of modern management and design theories.

In general, the book seeks to provide: 1) a sound introduction to the motel business; 2) the necessary concepts and principles of intelligent planning; 3) a guide to obtaining greatest value from investments in motel land, buildings, and facilities; and 4) a compilation of tried and proven methods and practices of proficient motel management.

Credit goes to the many motel managers, specialists, and designers who helped make this book possible with their generous contribution of comments, research data, and illustrations. Special thanks go to Dr. Kemper Merriam, motel accounting specialist, University of Arizona; William Johnson, landscape architect, Ann Arbor; Aarre Lahti, professor of design, University of Michigan; George Lytle, architect, Royal Oak, Michigan; and Kim Jepson, advertising specialist, Lansing. The authors are especially indebted to William C. Brown, who initially suggested the writing of this book. And the many hours of typing assistance by Beverly Snyder are sincerely appreciated.

Clare A. Gunn
Robert W. McIntosh

Contents

PART III   SUCCESSFUL MANAGEMENT

MOTEL PLANNING AND BUSINESS MANAGEMENT

PART I

Preliminary
Investigation

If one has a burning desire to own, manage, or build a motel where does one start? Too often, past motels have been started in the middle and have ended up in a muddle. This is not to deny that some have succeeded with little forethought or sound planning. But these are the exceptions. And who knows how much more successful even they would be if established on a more sound basis.

Before we are ready for architects and building contractors or even mortgagors, management must make major decisions about the business anticipated. Is the owner confident that this is the best place to put his money? Are the owners and managers confident that they are capable of establishing such an enterprise and making it a success? What is involved in establishing a new motel? Should you buy, or is it better to build a new one? What about the many lease arrangements now open to new developers? Are motels always profitable?

The discussions in this part of the book should be sobering to those inclined to take a flighty look at the purchase, building, or operating of a motel. Success is not so much a matter of big business versus little business but the better businessman versus the poor.

CHAPTER 1

Is This Business
for You?

Nobody would consider renting an office and proclaiming himself a barber, an accountant, a pharmacist or a photographer if he had had no training and was not qualified.

For some mysterious reason, however, thousands of people have declared themselves to be motel managers without any experience or training in this field. Motel management to them appears to be really quite simple and requires only that the person "like people" and be able to make beds and clean floors. *This is a gross oversimplification and an utterly false conception.* The fact that a few with unusual talents and great intestinal fortitude have succeeded on such a bulldozing approach is no proof that it is a desirable approach.

Actually, motel management in all of its important concepts is a very complex occupation. It requires a much broader range of skills and abilities than that of most other small businesses. The smaller the motel, the more of these skills must actually be performed by the manager. In a large place many of these can be done by hiring specially skilled persons such as building engineers or administrative housekeepers. But the motel manager himself must understand all of the functions of motel operation.

Successful motel management involves a fundamental understanding and knowledge of: (1) Building planning and the supervision of remodeling, construction, upgrading, and refurnishing. (2) Grounds development, parking, walks, drives, patios, and plant materials. (3) Advertising and sales techniques including public relations. (4) Front office management, reservations, deposits, office systems. (5) Guest courtesy, hospitality and entertainment. (6) Housekeeping and cleanliness. (7) Repairs and maintenance. (8) Laundry. (9) Interior decoration and furnishings. (10) Accounting, analysis of financial statements, taxes and personnel records. (11) Personnel training and supervision and (12) Laws and regulations of various levels of government as they pertain to this business.

This is a formidable list. Professional and specialized assistance will be needed in all or part of these success factors, but good judgment and common sense play an important role in the creation of a skilled motel manager. Education is essential to success and is a continuous process of inquiry and study throughout life. The alert manager constantly searches for new and improved ways of providing better and more satisfying service, thereby increasing and sustaining the profits of the business. Thus he is ever alert to suggestions and ideas which can be put to work.

Check yourself on these important qualifications:

1. Are you an improvement-minded person? Are you open to sub-gestions and eager to obtain new concepts and better methods for the improvement of your motel?
2. Can you effectively direct the work of others and build loyalty and respect from your staff?
3. Do you enjoy meeting the public and entertaining guests? Can you smile when you don't feel like smiling?
4. Are you in good health, vigorous, with plenty of energy?
5. Do you have good taste in color, design, materials, fabrics, and linens, or know enough to hire others if this is not your talent?
6. Can you stand late hours and frequent interruptions in your meals and sleeping hours?
7. Do you mind confinements? The motel business is probably the most confining of all small businesses. It is a 7-day week business, open 24 hours per day, 365 days each year. Some motels close for a vacation period when business is slow but during the busy period of the year there is no let-up.
8. In small motels, cleaning rooms, making beds, keeping records, supervising housekeeping and similar duties are tasks usually assigned to the wife. Does she object to such tasks?
9. Do you have high standards? This applies to the cleanliness of rooms, personal appearance, and moral standards. Motel rooms

are traditionally maintained at levels much higher than those in the typical American home.

10. Are you promotion-minded? In this business you must have self-confidence and be willing to spend money to advertise and sing the praises of your place. You must use your imagination to develop effective advertising and promotion techniques. Motel trade, endorsing convention and advertising associations deserve your support, as well as the chamber of commerce or other local booster organizations.

If you feel that you possess these attributes to a high degree you have the basic personal resources to make a satisfying and rewarding career in the motel field. If you feel somewhat inadequate in various aspects do not jump into the business. If you still desire to enter it, there are many opportunities to study, to improve and remove your deficiencies. These include short courses, conferences, institutes, home study courses, personal improvement courses, college courses and inservice training. These are outlined in more detail in the last chapter of this book under the heading "Proficiency in Management."

CHAPTER 2

Establishing
the New Business

How does one know a new business is needed? The term, "over-building," recently has become synonymous with motels, yet new ones are built daily—and ironically seem to succeed. Can this be predetermined? Perhaps it can, but even little understanding of the business is sufficient to show that there are many variables, any one of which can push toward either success or failure. This discussion therefore should not leave the implication that establishing a new motel follows an orderly or scientific approach, assuring success if properly followed. On the other hand, a few basics seem to favor success and to this end, the following material is presented.

First, is there need for new facilities in the proposed location? It is doubtful if the existing motel managers, service station attendants, or the chamber of commerce can give straight answers, although their comments might be enlightening. At the outset, one must realize that this question involves two aspects of motel offerings: *quality* and *quantity*. For example, a community may appear to have a surplus of rooms, but closer scrutiny could reveal the need for more rooms, but of a different degree of luxury or simplicity.

Among the first steps is study of the nature of the "generators" of overnight trade and how well these are being satisfied with present accommodations. A study of the community generators would reveal all those activities which attract people to the community—and rarely is a new motel on this list! Many owners are just now beginning to realize that simply building a motel of itself does not generate business. Among generators of overnight trade are hospitals, colleges, universities, business centers, industries, resort attractions, government agencies, and travel exchange points. Have these expanded or increased in numbers over the last few years? Have they declined or remained about the same? This gives some clue regarding the need for more accommodations.

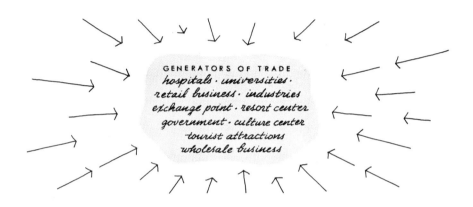

GENERATORS OF TRADE
hospitals · universities · retail business · industries exchange point · resort center government · culture center tourist attractions wholesale business

A next step is to determine the number and quality of accommodations in the community at the present time. This is often quite revealing. It sometimes shows that the number of rooms available has increased 5 per cent over 20 years, while the business and industrial expansion have been 150 per cent and furthermore, that the vast majority of the accommodations are of a pre-depression quality. On the contrary, it sometimes shows that the number of recent motel constructions has kept good pace with the community's economic growth. While direct numerical results cannot be obtained from this analysis, it does provide just one more clue to the need for a new motel, and also something about the character of offerings most needed.

In a way, this is performing a "market analysis," a term used to describe a systematic and intensive investigation to determine the market, more generally used in the development and sale of consumer goods. Some of these principles are being applied to motels and some of the motel chains make very complete depth studies of this kind. Normally, these are beyond the ability and experience of the novice motel owner or manager and the service should be obtained by those competent in this work.

Generally, market analyses involve both qualitative and quantitative studies. Listed below is some of the information a qualitative study would reveal:

1. Attitudes of the traveling public towards motels.
2. Trends in the motel industry.
3. Habits of motel guests—what influences them to choose one motel in preference to another motel or a hotel.
4. Reasons why people would want to stay at the motel.
5. Type of guests—age, occupation, sex, traveling habits, and income groups.
6. Seasonal aspects of the business—highs and lows (on weekly and yearly basis).
7. Prices or rates guests would be willing to pay.
8. Mode of guest travel—auto, plane, train, bus, boat.
9. Highway pattern and future highway changes, if any.
10. Existing competition in the community, and the quality of that competition.
11. What reasons guests would have for visiting your city—business, recreation, culture, education, scientific, entertainment, group function, social, transient.
12. To what extent food, beverages, or other service facilities should be offered.
13. Guest preferences for credit facilities, telephones, radios, television, swimming pools, and patios.
14. Where guests would come from—geographic distribution.
15. The most effective type of advertising program to use in reaching prospective guests.
16. Whether to make the motel a part of a chain, franchise, endorsing, referral or partnership organization.

The quantitative analysis of the market studies the buying power of the prospective motel and estimates the number of rooms, seats in the dining room, capacity of meeting rooms and other services. Information from such a study often shows:

1. A forecast of the motel's room sales, food and beverage sales for the first two years.
2. Where and when advertising can be used most productively.
3. Sales potentials (needed in order to measure managerial sales efficiency).
4. Population trends in prime market areas.

5. Commercial travelers and family expenditures for lodging and food, and the trends thereof.
6. Consumer incomes and trends in discretionary income.

The methods used in market research are not always the same but generally include some survey research, observation, and review of existing information. The technology of modern survey research is a far cry form early poll-taking, popular with voting predictions in years past. Complete review will not be given here, but the steps usually include determination of the population (the people to be covered in the survey); selection of the sample; interviewing; processing the data; and analyzing the results.

The astute market analyst gains much by experience. Often an outsider, with a critical and analytical eye, can see more about our business than we can even though we are with it every day. He has a certain objectivity and is unhampered by routine of a specific situation. He can place it in perspective of other similar business situations. His opinion and special study therefore are extremely valuable.

Many practical suggestions regarding market analysis are found in the booklet *What's New In Hotel Sales!* published by the Hotel Sales Management Association. Libraries often carry informative books and papers on market research performed by governmental agencies, colleges and universities, marketing journals, and sources such as *Survey of Buying Power*, published by Sales Management, Inc. Motel trade associations and publishers of trade journals periodically make market studies which are particularly helpful. Surveys of travel, such as those made by Curtis Publishing Company, the National Association of Travel Organizations, and *Wall Street Journal*, can be very helpful when reviewed and interpreted by the qualified person.

CHAPTER 3

Build, Buy, or Lease?

Whether to build, buy or lease is a fundamental consideration. Let's examine some of the important factors involved.

BUILDING A MOTEL

Probably most people think first of building a new motel rather than buying.

Advantages of Building

1. ARCHITECTURAL DESIGN. Newly constructed motels which have attractively designed buildings and grounds tend to have greater sales appeal than older places. Taste changes, and motels built today usually look quite different from those of 10 to 15 years ago. Thus if you build, your motel should be in style and have a good sales appeal longer than a motel already built.

2. SUITABILITY. Usually a new facility can better satisfy a now known demand than one built to a trade of the past.

3. LOCATION. Sometimes a location better suited to modern demand can be found by starting from the ground up.

4. FURNISHINGS. All new furnishings of the latest design can be installed at the outset; this gives customers a feeling of satisfaction on having chosen this "beautiful new motel."

Disadvantages of Building

1. COST. It takes a lot of ready cash to build and equip a new motel today. Also, a considerable sum is likely to be needed to carry along the operation before sufficient trade is established to make it pay its own way and return a profit.

2. TIME ELEMENT. A new motel will probably take from 12 to 18 months to become established. This means lack of income with its associated financial problems for a period of time.

BUYING A MOTEL

Advantages of Buying

Buying a well-located motel, which is in good condition, has several advantages:

1. LOCATION. By purchasing an established motel, you may have a better location than on open land for new building.

2. COMPETITION. A better competitive position may be found with a well established motel.

3. GOODWILL. Existing goodwill and patronage already accustomed to staying at the motel make an assured income available right away. Otherwise, it will take time to build up a trade. This is especially true where commercial travelers make up an important part of the trade.

4. FINANCING. It depends upon the individual circumstance, but sometimes you can buy a motel with less cash than building. A land contract with the previous owner is an example.

Disadvantages of Buying

Certain disadvantages of buying must be recognized.

1. DESIGN AND CONSTRUCTION. There may be features in design or construction which are not particularly appealing to today's guests and which soon require replacement for sound construction.

2. WHAT'S UNDERGROUND? Underground service facilities such as a well or waste disposal system may be in poor condition. If reconstruction appears imminent, such costs should be added to purchase price.

3. HIGHWAY RELOCATION. A highway relocation project might be in the planning stage; this could drastically affect the future of the business.

4. PAST REPUTATION. It may take some time to correct an unfavorable reputation created by a previous owner.

LEASING

Not very many motels are leased, but leasing may become more common in the future. Considerations, both favorable and unfavorable, are:

1. LOWEST INVESTMENT. Much less capital is needed to lease. An advance rental of 1 or 2 years is often required, but this is much smaller than the cost of buying or building a motel.

2. DURATION OF LEASE. Advantages depend mostly on "the times" and the rental may become too low or too high over inflationary or deflationary periods. A short-term lease will give you a sample of life as a motel keeper and you could get out of it at the end of the lease if desired.

3. LESS RISK. As you don't have as much money tied up, you may expect to lose less if business fails or doesn't come up to expectations.

4. THE MOTEL STILL ISN'T YOURS. If you are a good motel operator you will build up an excellent business as a lessee. Over a period of years you have paid your rent or percentage of net profit or gross revenue, but you still don't own the motel and you can't take advantage of an opportunity to sell at a profit.

5. BUT YOU'VE HAD EXCELLENT EXPERIENCE. You may want to buy out the original owner or build a new motel for yourself after your experience as a lessee.

SALE—LEASEBACK

This is a device which provides the owner of a motel with additional capital for expansion and upgrading (which he may have been unable to provide by his own funds or through normal loaning agencies). To raise this capital, he sells the motel and at the same time negotiates a long-term net lease with the new owner. The terms of the lease usually allow the seller undisturbed continuation of the operation of the business. The new owner's interest in the motel is concerned only with his annual rental collection. The lessor (new owner) is an investor exclusively and not a motel operator.

The net lease requires the lessee (the one who leases, sometimes called a tenant) to pay the following:

1. All operating expenses
2. Real estate taxes
3. Complete maintenance of the property

All items which are paid for by the lessee are currently deductible for income tax purposes as a regular business expense.

The lessor pays only the mortgage carrying charges if the property was purchased with a mortgage. Leases usually run from 15 to 25 years and most of them have renewal options.

INVESTMENT IN LAND

In all of these considerations, the tax angle must be carefully reviewed. Under present federal income tax regulations, the portion of your investment in the land is not depreciable. This amount cannot be recovered unless the motel is sold. An alternative to buying the land is to lease it. Your annual rental payment for the land is currently deductible as a business expense and the money which might have been invested in the land can be used for other aspects of the motel business. However, a loan is more difficult to negotiate for a motel investment on leased land, and in many instances, is impossible. This depends on the situation and location. A very favorable location might ease this situation, but loaning agencies generally are most reluctant to loan where leased land is involved.

CAPITAL IMPROVEMENTS

Most people who invest in a motel soon see the need for improvements which they feel are needed to increase patronage. Financing of these betterments is usually made from current earnings, short-term loans or credit. The short-term effect of these expenditures tends to reduce profits. Thus, a very common experience for new motel operators is to find that they have a very small profit—or none at all—for the first year or so.

In lease arrangements, the lessee may likewise make capital improvements. These are amortized as leasehold improvements, usually for the life of the lease.

MOTEL APPRAISAL

The determination of a motel's market value requires a somewhat complicated procedure. A qualified real estate appraiser having experience with motels is best able to provide the most accurate figure.

Basically, the appraisal method is as follows:

1. A careful evaluation is made of the motel location, site, physical conditions and prospects for future business, including present and likely future competition.

2. The physical or replacement value is determined by arriving at the sum of the following:
   (a) value of the land occupied by the motel
   (b) cost of land improvements
   (c) buildings (less depreciation)
   (d) furnishings and equipment (less depreciation)

3. Next, a capitalization of estimated excess profits (if any) is added. This excess profit figure is the amount of profit in excess of the amount which is considered normal for motel operations. As an example, if the normal return is considered as 10 per cent of capital investment as shown on the balance sheet and the excess profit situation could reasonably be expected to continue for 3 years, then a 30 per cent capitalization rate would be used. To illustrate: If the excess profit was $2,100, then the amount to be added would be computed by dividing $2,100 by 30 per cent which would be $7,000. This would then be added to the foregoing amounts in arriving at the fair market value.

4. Finally, 10 per cent of the replacement or physical value is added to obtain the sale or economic value.

Example of motel appraisal:

a.	Value of land occupied by motel	$ 22,000
b.	Cost of land improvements	7,000
c.	Cost of buildings, less depreciation	67,000
d.	Cost of furnishings and equipment, less depreciation	8,000
e.	Capitalization of estimated excess profit	7,000
f.[1]	Add 10% of replacement value	10,400
	Sale or economic value	$121,400

Market or sale value is also affected by the *terms* of the sale. If a long-term land contract or mortgage can be negotiated, the buyer is likely to pay more than if he has a high cash down payment and is to clear the obligation in a relatively short repayment period.

---

[1]This figure comprises 10 per cent of the sum of items a, b, c, & d.

CHAPTER 4

Patterns
of Ownership

FRANCHISES

The day and age of the brand names is here and will no doubt stay. Nationally advertised products with their standard trademarks and signs are seen wherever business is conducted. The franchise motel thus gains some advantage over an individually designed motel because the traveler is familiar with the standardized sign and the motel's distinctive exterior appearance. If standards slip in one motel of a brand, however, many others will be damaged businesswise.

A franchise is a contractual arrangement whereby the company owning the franchise gives permission to a local investor to use the company's architectural design, sign, standardized furnishings and rather specific operating methods. The local investor may or may not operate the motel. This depends on the particular circumstances of each proposition and the policies of each company. In any event, the person who invests in the motel pays a certain fee to the franchising company, usually computed as a percentage of the gross revenue. The local investor feels that this fee is worth its cost due to the increased business which allegedly is generated because of the fame of the franchising company and the assurance in the prospective guest's mind that he will receive fair value for his dollar.

Some well known national franchising companies are Holiday Inns of America, Inc., Howard Johnson's Motor Lodges, Quality Courts Motels, Inc. and Congress Motels.

LEASES

In a lease arrangement, a local investor builds a motel and then leases it to another party who becomes the operator. Ordinarily, a standard architectural design is not employed. One company may operate many different motels on a lease basis, but the properties do not look alike. This is a typical arrangement in hotel companies. A company may lease motels from local owners and then combine these properties into their chain organization. Examples are the Albert Pick Hotels, Inc., and Western International Hotels.

In the usual lease arrangement, the local investor provides the land and the building. The lessee (who leases the property from the lessor) provides the furnishings, linens, and equipment necessary for the motel's operation. A definite period of time is specified, often 10 years. Lease payments can be of two types: a flat fee paid in regular installments or a percentage lease, usually on a graduated scale, based upon the gross volume of business. Sometimes a combination of the two methods is used. The lease is usually written so that it can be renewed after the initial period.

By leasing his property, the local investor is relieved of the responsibility of the daily operation of the motel and at the same time receives a steady return on his investment. The lessee has the opportunity of showing what he can do to run a profitable business, with a minimum of investment. Thus, the lease arrangement is of mutual advantage and usually provides the guest with a larger, more elaborate and better managed motel than might be the case with local capital and talent.

CHAINS OR MOTEL SYSTEMS

A chain or motel system company owns several different properties. According to the American Hotel and Motel Association, such a company must own at least three different properties before it is recognized as a chain. There are now over 40 hotel chains in the United States and this development is one of the most significant in the industry since 1945.

Motel chains are not numerous. Two of the largest chains are Holiday Inns of America, Inc., which also has franchises and the TraveLodge Corp., which has a partnership arrangement. In effect, motel franchise companies such as Howard Johnson's are chains.

PARTNERSHIPS

The high cost of motel construction has brought about the need for more capital. One of the ways to provide this is to enter into a partnership. Each partner could be active in the management or one partner could actually manage the business and the other partner (s) could remain silent. Profits are divided according to the equity of each partner.

At least two motel chain companies, TraveLodge and Imperial 400, have a 50-50 partnership arrangement for providing capital. The local partner has full responsibility for management and operation. This system is based on the supposition that a motel twice as large as a local investor could build would do more than twice the business of a smaller motel. Present trends toward the more elaborate motor hotels would tend to bear this out.

Sometimes a man and wife enter into a formal business partnership. This has some financial advantages in regard to Social Security, if the earnings of each partner are sufficiently high. There do not appear to be any other advantages, as the income tax liability would be the same as if the business were a single proprietorship.

One other matter deserves mention in regard to partnerships. Sometimes the opinions of the partners differ widely after the business becomes well established. This may cause a rift which can be solved only by one partner's buying out the other (s) and assuming sole responsibility for management.

CORPORATION

The main advantage of a corporate type organization is that it provides limited liability in case the business should suffer reverses or be sued for a large sum. The liability of each stockholder is limited to the amount of his investment in the corporation.

Raising capital by selling stock is a common method of securing funds for any business and is equally so for motels. After the business becomes established, the earned surplus is distributed to the stockholders in accordance with their share holdings.

A new provision of the federal income tax gives a corporation the privilege of being taxed as a partnership or a corporation, whichever is to the advantage of the corporation. In corporations, the first $25,000 of profit is taxed at a normal rate of 30 per cent and all earnings over $25,000 are taxed at 52 per cent. The new provisions thus are flexible and of advantage to this business.

To attract capable young managerial talent, such as a graduate of a college hotel management course, a motel corporation could offer him shares. He can thus earn his salary, perhaps a bonus, and buy shares of the corporation. In fact, some corporations can make a very attractive offer to a promising young man by assuring him that he can gradually acquire stock until he is the principal stockholder when the original stockholders are less interested in the business than they were at the beginning.

CHAPTER 5

Revenue and Expense Estimates

Careful estimates of revenue and expense should be made when a new motel is in the blueprint stage and before any financial obligations of consquence have been incurred. These estimates should include rate structure, percentage of occupancy, distribution of major expense items, return on investment, repayment on the mortgage, and estimated federal and state taxes.

This is the point in the planning process when the prospective owner should make as complete an investigation as possible and do some hardheaded thinking. The wise investor estimates revenue lower than he thinks it might be and vice versa as to expenses. It is better to be pleasantly surprised than to be bitterly disappointed.

ESTIMATING REVENUE

We recommended that annual gross room revenues be estimated on a *per room basis*. This amount could range from say $800 to $3,500 per room per year. Gross room revenues of $2,000 to $3,000 per year are considered to be excellent. Room revenue is a function of two factors—*average room rate* and *percentage of occupancy*. The more persons who occupy a room, the higher the average rate. If your motel is expected to accommodate a large percentage of tourists, then the chances are that you will have a considerably higher average room rate than the commercial-type motel which caters largely to single business travelers.

Average room rate is computed over a given period by dividing the gross room revenues by the number of rooms which are occupied.

Percentage of occupancy is the other key to success. It should be as high as possible. Occupancy percentage is computed by dividing the number of rooms which are rented, over a given period of time, by the total number of rooms which were available for rent during this same period. In motel circles, there is a universal feeling that the property must be rented at a level of at least 70 per cent occupancy to achieve a reasonable profit. An occupancy of 60 per cent is often considered as the break-even point, so profits are obtained only beyond this figure. These percentages are general averages, however, and should not be considered as absolute. Some smaller family motels can make profits at occupancies lower than 60 per cent and others may not be profitable at even much higher occupancies.

ESTIMATING EXPENSES

Studies of many hundreds of revenue and expense statements by these authors since 1946 indicate that a reasonably successful, efficiently operated motel will net from 10 to 30 per cent of gross revenue before federal income taxes. This net figure actually consists of two amounts:

1. Return to the owner as interest on his equity capital and
2. Return to the owner for his labor and management.

Thus, until the return equity capital is removed from the net profit figure, the actual return to the owner is likely to appear deceptively high. Studies by the *Tourist Court Journal* show that the interest on owner's equity is less than half of the net profit figures and somewhat over half constitutes the owner's return for labor and management.

The accompanying tables on motel operations are the results of nationwide studies by three leading sources. Review of these should prove enlightening to both the novice and experienced motel man. Since these data change annually, the most recent information can be obtained directly from the sources.

National Motel Expense Ratios[1]

Motel Operations—As Reported
In *Tourist Court Journal*

1961

INCOME:
Room Rentals	86.23%
Coffee Room	11.72%
Sundry Sales	.47%
Other Income	.90%
Rents, Concessions, etc.	.68%
	100.00%

OPERATING EXPENSES:
Salaries and Wages	18.78%
Executive Salaries	4.39%
Laundry	4.55%
Linen, China, Glassware	1.33%
Advertising, Ptg. & Sta.	4.57%
Payroll Taxes, Insurance	2.73%
Heat, Light and Power	6.14%
Repairs and Maintenanec	4.04%
Cleaning and Other Supplies	1.50%
Telephone and Telegraph	1.59%
Other Operating Expenses	2.93%
Total Operating Expenses	52.55%
GROSS OPERATING PROFIT	47.45%

CAPITAL EXPENSES:
Real Estate and Prop. Taxes	3.65%
Insurance	1.06%
Interest	7.27%
Rent	5.77%
Depreciation and Amortization	19.70%
Total Capital Expenses	37.45%
NET PROFIT	10.00%
INTEREST ON OWNER'S EQUITY	4.29%
OWNER'S RETURN FOR LABOR AND MANAGEMENT	5.71%

AVERAGE INVESTMENT PER MOTEL:
Buildings	$156,625
Furniture and Fixtures	47,960
Subtotal	$204,585
Land	24,800
Total Investment	$229,385

GENERAL STATISTICS:
Average No. Rooms per Motel	35
Percentage of Occupancy	69.91%
Average Daily Rate per Rented Room	$8.40
Average Daily Rate per Guest	$4.68
Average No. Guests per Room	1.80

[1] Copyright July 1962 issue *Tourist Court Journal,* Temple, Texas. Further reproduction in part or in whole prohibited unless written permisson obtained from the copyright owner.

Motor Hotel Operations—As Reported
by Horwath & Horwath[2]

	Ratios to Room Sales	
	No. Operated	*Restaurant*
	Restaurant 1961	*Operated 1961*
INCOME:		
Guest room rentals	100.00%	100.00%
Public room rentals	N[3]	1.0[3]
Restaurant		
Operating profit		18,2
Lease income	5.2[3]	
Other income (net)	2.1	3.2
Total	105.1%	121.4%
OPERATING EXPENSES:		
Payroll	24.3%	27.4%
Payroll taxes and employee relations	2.1	2.4
Total	26.4%	29.8%
Housekeeping	8.7	9.5
Administrative and general	6.3	7.5
Advertising	4.6	5.2
Heat, light and power	5.0	6.7
Repairs and maintenance	3 8	5.3
Total	54.8%	64.0%
HOUSE PROFIT, (BEFORE TAXES,		
INTEREST, DEPRECIATION, ETC.)	50.3%	57.4%
Percentage of occupancy	71.55%	72.17%
Ratio to total sales including restaurant		
rental income and other income		
Payroll (including restaurant)	21.8%	27.1%
Payroll taxes and employee relations	1.9	2.5
Total	23.7%	29.6%
Administrative and general	5.6	3.6
Advertising	4.1	2.5
Heat, light and power	4.5	3.2
Repairs and maintenance	3.4	2.6
House profit	45.1	27.8

[2] Reproduced by permission of Horwath & Horwath, copyright owners.

[3] Average only of those motor hotels having rental income from public rooms and/or leased restaurant.

Motor Hotels with Restaurants—As Reported
by Harris, Kerr, and Forster[4]

	All Motor Hotels With Restaurants —1961	Size Per Motor Hotel —1961	
		Under 100 Rooms	Over 100 Rooms
TOTAL SALES AND INCOME:			
Rooms	49.7%	53.9%	48.7%
Food	36.1	34.8	36.4
Beverages	10.2	8.0	10.7
Telephone	2.9	2.6	3.0
Other Departmental Profits	.2	.1	.2
Other Income	.9	.6	1.0
Total	100.0%	100.0%	100.0%
COST OF GOODS SOLD AND DEPARTMENTAL WAGES AND EXPENSES:			
Rooms	13.7%	16.0%	13.2%
Food and Beverages	38.2	36.4	38.6
Telephone	3.6	3.0	3.7
Total	55.5%	55.4%	55.5%
GROSS OPERATING INCOME:	44.5%	44.6%	44.5%
DEDUCTIONS FROM INCOME:			
Administrative and General Expenses	8.2%	9.6%	7.9%
Advertising and Sales Promotion	2.9	3.1	2.9
Heat, Light and Power	4.1	4.9	3.9
Repair and Maintenance	3.5	3.7	3.5
Total	18.7%	21.3%	18.2%
HOUSE PROFIT	25.8%	23.3%	26.3%
STORE RENTALS	.4	.1	.5
GROSS OPERATING PROFIT	26.2%	23.4%	26.8%
FIRE INSURANCE AND FRANCHISE TAXES	.6	.9	.5
PROFIT BEFORE REAL ESTATE AND OTHER CAPITAL EXPENSES	25.6%	22.5%	26.3%
REAL ESTATE TAXES	2.7	2.6	2.8
PROFIT AFTER REAL ESTATE TAXES BUT BEFORE OTHER CAPITAL EXPENSES[5]	22.9%	19.9%	23.5%
PERCENTAGE OF OCCUPANCY	72.3%	70.6%	72.8%
AVERAGE RATE PER ROOM PER DAY	$ 9.72	$ 9.40	$ 9.81
AVERAGE DAILY ROOM RATE PER GUEST	$ 6.61	$ 6.27	$ 6.70
NUMBER OF GUESTS PER OCCUPIED ROOM	1.47	1.50	1.46
TIMES REAL ESTATE TAXES EARNED	9.4	8.5	9.6
AVERAGE SIZE (ROOMS)	125	67	167

[4] Reproduced by permission of Harris, Kerr, and Forster, copyright owners.

[5] Profit Before Deducting Depreciation, Rent, Interest, Amortization and Income Taxes.

Motor Hotels with Restaurants—As Reported
by Harris, Kerr, and Forster

	All Motor Hotels With Restaurants —1961	Size Per Motel Hotel —1961	
		Under 100 Rooms	Over 100 Rooms
ROOMS:			
Net Sales:			
Guests' Rooms	99.3%	99.9%	99.1%
Public Rooms	.7	.1	.9
Total Sales	100.0%	100.0%	100.0%
Departmental Expenses:			
Salaries and Wages Including			
Vacation	16.3%	17.7%	16.0%
Employees' Meals	.5	1.0	.5
Payroll Taxes and Employee			
Relations	1.4	1.3	1.4
Laundry	3.5	4.0	3.3
Linen, China and Glass	1.2	.9	1.2
Other Expenses	4.7	4.9	4.6
Total Expenses	27.6%	29.8%	27.0%
Departmental Profit	72.4%	70.2%	73.0%
FOOD AND BEVERAGES:			
Food Sales	100.0%	100.0%	100.0%
Cost of Food Consumed	43.9%	47.4%	43.1%
Less: Employees' Meals	5.1	5.7	5.0
Cost of Food Sold	38.8%	41.7%	38.1%
Food Gross Profit	61.2%	58.3%	61.9%
Beverage Sales	100.0%	100.0%	100.0%
Cost of Beverages Sold	31.0	36.0	30.1
Beverage Gross Profit	69.0%	64.0%	69.9%
Total Food and Beverage Sales	100.0%	100.0%	100.0%
Cost of Food and Beverages Sold	37.1	40.7	36.3
Food and Beverage Gross Profit	62.9%	59.3%	63.7%
Departmental Expenses			
Salaries and Wages Including			
Vacation	30.5%	29.6%	30.6%
Employees' Meals	2.8	2.7	2.8
Payroll Taxes and Employee			
Relations	2.5	2.1	2.8
Music and Entertainment	1.4	1.4	1.3
Laundry	1.7	2.1	1.6
Kitchen Fuel	.5	.8	.5
Linen	.3	.2	.3
China and Glass	1.1	.9	1.1
Silver	.3	.2	.4
Menus and Drink Lists	.4	.4	.4
Licenses and Taxes	.2	.4	.2
Other Epenses	3.8	3.6	3.8
Total Expenses	45.5%	44.4%	45.8%
Departmental Profit	17.4%	14.9%	17.9%
Average Receipt per Food Cover	$1.64	$1.43	$1.69

AVERAGE OPERATING RESULTS[6]

	Motels 1-10 units Percent	Motels 11-20 units Percent	Motels 21-40 units Percent
INCOME:			
Room rentals	95.98	94.31	96.40
Coffee rooms		4.09	2.00
Sundry sales	.18	.20	.47
Rents and concessions	1.17	.53	.34
Other income	2.67	.87	.79
Total income	100.00	100.00	100.00
OPERATING EXPENSES:			
Salaries and wages	7.62	11.48	15.56
Executive salaries		2.46	3.15
Laundry	5.52	4.50	4.60
Linen, chinaware, glassware	1.35	1.07	1.00
Advertising, printing, stationery	2.85	3.04	3.98
Payroll, taxes, insurance	1.66	1.46	1.79
Heat, light and power	9.46	7.45	7.01
Repairs and maintenance	3.50	4.45	4.48
Cleaning and other supplies	.82	1.48	1.73
Telephone and telegraph	2.05	2.31	1.87
Other operating expenses	2.58	2.62	2.46
Total operating expenses	37.41	42.32	47.63
Gross operating profit	62.59	57.68	52.37
CAPITAL EXPENSES:			
Real estate and property taxes	4.24	4.37	3.79
Insurance	1.73	1.65	1.47
Interest	6.34	8.35	8.91
Rent	1.25	1.11	2.59
Depreciation	27.84	17.47	20.50
Total capital expenses	41.40	32.95	37.26
Net profit	21.19	24.73	15.11
AVERAGE INVESTMENT PER MOTEL:			
Buildings	$35,000	$70,785	$133,705
Furniture and fixtures	7,720	16,420	35.895
Subtotal	42,720	87,205	169,600
Land	7,430	15,765	22.950
Total investment	50,150	102,970	192.550
GENERAL STATISTICS:			
Percentage of occupancy (percent)	64,14	68.43	71.35
Average daily rate per rented room	$6.05	$7.19	$7.65
Average daily rate per guest	$3.47	$3.87	$4.01
Average number guests per room	1.75	1.85	1.90

[6] Reproduced from Small Business Administration Publication, 1963, *Starting and Managing a Small Motel,* by Harold Whittington.

If you hire a manager, the percentage of net income is very likely to be lower. In fact, the larger the motel, the lower the *percentage* of net income. The dollar amounts would likely be higher, however. In a husband-and-wife operation where there is very little hired labor, the percentage of net income from operations would consequently be higher.

DETERMINING RATES—SOME THOUGHTS

Determining the motel's rate structure is vital because the financial success of the business depends heavily upon room revenues.

There are two schools of thought on rates. A progressive school holds that rates bear no relationship to costs. The rate should be set at what the room is worth and what the guest is willing to pay. For example, various embellishments can be provided in guest rooms which make them appear rich and comfortable. In the mind of the guest, he expects the room to be more expensive than the usual room and is willing to pay for it. The *investment* in the room may not be high; it just *appears* that way. The same principle can be applied to the motel's exterior appearance, lawn, grounds, or lobby. Imaginative design and skillful blending of the building components using lower cost materials can produce a motel which has excellent aesthetic appeal, but actually represents a modest investment. The owner of such a motel makes a better than average profit because he has an attractive motel—yet a low investment per room. *In the final analysis, the rates would have to cover costs but the costs are not the basis for computing rates.*

The other school of thought concerning rates holds that the average rate charged should represent the costs involved in providing the room, plus overhead, return on investment and a fair compensation to the owner for his labor and management. Thus, rates are computed on the basis of costs and a fair profit. The choice is one each manager must make for himself. The authors favor the progressive school as it is more likely to yield a greater profit and in periods when higher rates are impossible to obtain, can be flexible and lowered to meet these conditions.

The following form can be used to compute rates based on the costs-return method:

Rate Computation by Costs—Returns Method

Amount

CONTROLLABLE OPERATING EXPENSES:
Owner's and/or manager's salaries .... $————————
Employees' wages .... ————————
Payroll taxes and employee benefits .... ————————
    Total wage expense .... ————————
Laundry, dry cleaning and uniforms .... ————————
Linen costs .... ————————
Guest room supplies .... ————————
Cleaning supplies .... ————————
Advertising and sales promotion .... ————————
Commissions, discounts and allowances .... ————————
Dues, subscriptions and contributions .... ————————
Telephone, telegraph .... ————————
Office supplies, services, and postage .... ————————
Traveling and automobile expenses .... ————————
Fuel, water and electricity .... ————————
Repairs and maintenance .... ————————
Cash over and short .... ————————
Other operating expenses .... ————————
    Total controllable operating expenses ...... ————————

FIXED EXPENSES:
Rent—land and buildings .... ————————
Rent—equipment and furnishings .... ————————
Licenses and taxes .... ————————
Insurance .... ————————
Interest .... ————————
Depreciation and amortization .... ————————
    Total fixed expenses .... ————————

MANAGEMENT RETURN
Investments:
Land .... ————————
Improvements .... ————————
Buildings .... ————————
Furnishings & equipment .... ————————
TOTAL INVESTMENT .... ————————

Owner's equity .... ——————————
Interest on owner's equity ———% of $———
Owner's return for management .... ————————

    TOTAL MANAGEMENT RETURN ......

    TOTAL INCOME NEEDED ....

Computing rates:

Number of units available to rent ————————

Number of units available per year:

$$\frac{\qquad}{\text{Units}} \quad \text{x} \quad \frac{\qquad}{\text{Days}} \quad = \quad \frac{\qquad}{\text{Units available per year}}$$

(For estimating purposes, 70 per cent is commonly used in figuring occupancy.)

$$\frac{\qquad}{\text{\% Occupancy}} \quad \text{x} \quad \frac{\qquad}{\text{Units available per year}} \quad = \quad \frac{\qquad}{\text{Units rented per year}}$$

$$\frac{\$\qquad}{\text{Total income needed}} \quad \div \quad \frac{\qquad}{\text{Units rented per year.}} \quad = \quad \frac{\qquad}{\text{Av. rate per unit}}$$

OTHER METHODS OF ESTABLISHING RATES

Several other "methods" of determining rates are used by motel managers. The most common is to set rates similar to your competitors. This procedure is not recommended as it does not necessarily reflect true value received. Another is to vary the rate depending on the appearance of the prospect. This is wholly unethical. Rates should always be posted in every room. When they are, a guest knows that he has been charged the standard rate for the room, in accordance with the stated rate schedule.

Rates have steadily increased since 1955. Whereas the motel industry made its initial growth because of its convenience, no tipping, and rates lower than hotels, the present trend seems to be just the opposite. Rates are going up, tipping practices have crept in, and there seems to be less convenience at some motels now than formerly. Public acceptance of motels will remain at satisfactory levels only if true values are offered. Charging rates out of line with satisfactions received is the surest way to lose business.

CHAPTER 6

Related Supplemental Businesses

Profits of a motel can be increased by offering added services such as food, snacks, beverages, gifts, souvenirs, and sundry sales. In fact, such additional services often produce two-way benefits. The added services in themselves show a profit and at the same time, the motel occupancy rises because of the "package" offering of the motel.

RESTAURANT AND FOOD SERVICE

As a usual thing, a motel will do a better business if it can offer food service. People like to have such conveniences handy and if they have a choice of a motel with food as contrasted to one without, they will pick the one with the meal service.

Several alternatives are possible. If you can find a location adjacent to a first-rate restaurant, that's a big vote in favor of such a site. Lacking this, a restaurant can be built and operated by the motel. At this point a caution should be offered. Of all the over-all business operations, food service is most prone to failure. *Any food service operation must be evaluated on its own success factors.* Seldom can one motel's guests adequately support a restaurant. Another plan is to construct a restaurant and then lease it to a capable person or restaurant company. The final alternative is to have some very simple food service such as a continental breakfast or coffee shop. The continental breakfast can be set up with a minimum of investment: an automatic coffee maker activated by a time

29

clock; paper-lined cups which require no washing; powdered cream; and sugar lumps. Rolls can be under a glass cover to keep them sanitary. This arrangement requires very little labor and expense. If you have a good restaurant nearby, your offering of a continental breakfast is unwise. Better to build a cooperative relationship with the restaurant owner than to strain the feeling of goodwill by offering a free breakfast.

What Is Service?[1]

Restaurant service can be the target of complaints—or it can be the main drawing power of a successful operation. It can be bad or it can be good, but if you plan to stay in business there is no choice. . .it MUST be good. And if you plan to make yours a topnotch operation, it must be VERY good.

So, what is good restaurant service?

It is a composite of many things . . . little things, big things, tangibles, intangibles, details. It is inexpensive, but extremely valuable. It's an art, really . . . the art of being in the right place at the right time . . . the art of making every customer feel at home, welcome, and above all, important.

Good service is an immaculate uniform on a trim, pleasant waitress. It is a bowl of soup served piping hot and a glass of water served ice cold. It's a second glass of water, too . . . and a third. Or a second cup of coffee.

Good service is a touch of psychology, too . . . of sensing when a customer could use a spark of friendly conversation and when he wishes to be alone with his thoughts or with his companions. It is a warm smile of hospitality in greeting, a broad grin at a joke you've heard many times before, or a sympathetic understanding of a personal problem.

Good service is an attentive ear to an order and a careful pencil when jotting it down. It is helpful suggestions from the menu to an undecided customer and a courteous, accurate interpretation of an unfamiliar entree to a puzzled one. It is a close but unobtrusive observance of a customer's welfare . . . of his progress through the meal, his immediate needs, and his reaction to your treatment of him thus far.

Good service is a clean ashtray on a clean, uncluttered table . . . a matchbook or lighter within easy reach . . . a salt shaker, a sauce dispenser, an extra square of butter. It's a steak or a hamburger lying on a sparkling clean plate that is unmarred by chips or smudges . . . a soup spoon or a steak knife in its proper position . . . an extra roll or an olive. And it is

[1]By Edward J. Mayland

Food service, an increasing need at motels, can be closely integrated with the lodging, crisp and simply styled, as shown here. The Charterhouse Motel, *Annapolis; Victor Gruen,* architect.

A

B

For some trade a warm, rich and quiet decor is appropriate. Decorative divider at rear separates dining area from bar. Caravan Inn East, Phoenix, Arizona; *Ashton and Wilson, architects.*

C

To satisfy the widest range of patronage, the Maverick Room of the South Gate Motor Hotel, Arlington, offers a pleasing but simple decor. *Richard Parli, architect.*

the delightful surprise of an unexpected dash of whipped cream or a cherry atop a hot fudge sundae.

Good service is the placing of a noisy group of patrons at a discreet distance from the lone diner who may be wrestling with an important personal decision. It is the high chair and bib provided for the tot at another table. It is good lighting without glare . . . smooth efficiency of duty performed without an air of tension or undue effort . . . a fresh comfortable atmosphere that is conducive to calm, relaxed eating.

Despite its diversity, good service is surprisingly easy to recognize. Like the season of Spring, which is also a composite of countless factors both large and small, it's an over-all feeling . . . a mighty good feeling.

To the restaurant customer, it's the pot of gold at the end of the rainbow. And if he finds it at YOUR place of business, the search is over and he becomes a steady customer.

COCKTAIL LOUNGE

As regulated by state and local ordinance, the provision of a bar or cocktail lounge is ordinarily quite a profitable business compared to the investment and expense. Commercial travelers are especially good customers. Whether or not a cocktail lounge is included depends largely on the class of clientele and how well this provision is integrated with the food service. Some division from family dining areas is often desirable if not required by law.

GIFTS AND SOUVENIRS OR CURIOS

Many travelers like to purchase items as souvenirs or gifts. A gift shop can be a very delightful addition to a motel, if it is planned and operated by talented people who know this business. Every part of the country has its special allure. Crafts which are typical of the region can be effectively marketed in a motel. The gift shop is often placed near the lobby, office, or dining room so that it is convenient to the passing guests. Your nearest gift shop distributor can assist you in locating lines of merchandise.

OTHER POSSIBILITIES

Gross revenues can be supplemented by some other enterprises. These could include store or office rentals, day rentals, swimming pool patrons, miniature golf, bowling, coin operated vending machines, rental of office machines, gasoline station, rental of sports equipment, guided tours, sale of sundries—drugs, films, magazines, newspapers, and similar items.

CHAPTER 7

Financing

GROWING NEED FOR CAPITAL

More businesses fail due to underfinancing than probably any other cause. The day and age of "shoestring" operations is over. Motels are expensive to build and if they are to attract and satisfy sufficient customers to produce a profitable level of business, they must be designed and built properly. This takes ample capital. Today's concept of motel facilities involves a motel of sufficient size to present a substantial and attractive façade to the motorist as he slows down to examine the property.

Efficient and profitable motel management suggests a minimum of 20 rooms and probably 40 to 60 rooms or more would be better. As a part-time seasonal enterprise, any number of rooms might be feasible, depending on circumstances. Seldom can an owner receive enough income to justify an operation of 10 rooms or less. In addition, considerable capital is needed to meet customer demand for such niceties as a modern restaurant, lobby, cocktail lounge, swimming pool, patio, television, radios and telephones in the rooms as well as central heating and air conditioning.

In addition to the funds needed for land acquisition and construction, capital will be required for furnishings, linens (if not rented) and various items of equipment.

An additional 5 to 10 per cent of the total outlay should be provided as a cushion to meet operating expenses before the motel begins to pay its way.

EQUITY CAPITAL

An almost universal rule of commercial loaning agencies states that the owner should have about as much of his own money in the business as the lender is asked to provide. Exceptions to this rule may extend as much as 60-40 but by and large, a 50-50 situation prevails.

FINANCING

Your local bank is the most likely prospect for obtaining a loan. If your banker cannot make the loan, he is in a good position to suggest some other source. These may include insurance companies, trust companies, building and loan associations, partnerships, a corporation organization, and finally, the Small Business Administration. This is an agency of the United States government and will loan funds only when other commercial sources have failed. First mortgage loans can be made to motels for construction and upgrading. This may be a participation loan with a bank or a direct loan.

PROSPECTUS FOR MORTGAGE

A complete presentation for a loan helps in selling the bank on your application. This prospectus should include:

1. An analysis of the proposed location and site; both advantages and disadvantages for the intended use.

2. Proposed layout of all development, including buildings, drives, water supply, waste disposal, play areas, signs, waterfront development, etc.

3. Proposed building plans; at least rough floor plans and suggested exteriors with some notes about specifications.

4. Estimated costs of building construction, equipment, furnishings, and all site development—all the costs to get the business started.

5. A business prospectus—an estimate of fixed costs, operating costs, possible income and return on the investment.

6. Personal qualifications of the owners or managers; justification for your establishing this business.

REPAYMENT PERIOD

The most conservative arrangement is to write the mortgage for 10 years or longer. If possible, include an option to pay off this indebtedness whenever funds are available. So doing provides considerable freedom for the owner and relieves him of the pressure to pay large installments which may put a squeeze on the operation of the business.

RELATIONSHIP BETWEEN LOAN REPAYMENTS AND DEPRECIATION EXPENSE

Depreciation expense is a bookkeeping procedure which reduces the capital account and builds up the reserve for depreciation. Depreciation expense, of course, decreases the income tax liability because it reduces the net profit. The purpose of the allowance for this particular expense is to create a fund for the eventual replacement, enlargement, or modernization of the property. If funds equal to the depreciation allowance are used for repayment of the mortgage loan, these funds will not be available for replacement purposes as mentioned. Practical management expediency dictates however that depreciation reserve funds can be used for mortgage repayments—at least for the first few years. As soon as possible, however, loan repayment should be made out of earnings and a depreciation fund set aside to provide future improvements and eventual replacement of the property.

PART II

Building the
New Motel

Decisions on buildings are the most costly and enduring of all in the motel business. If we make a mistake in this year's advertising program or on today's menu in the coffee shop, it can be rectified next year or tomorrow without great cost. Not so with errors in location, site development or building design. As the years go by we are forced to live with the decisions made at the start—good or bad. If they were good decisions, the life of the business is extended; if not, it may be a losing proposition for present and all future owners, to say nothing of the adverse influence on the neighborhood and entire community.

This section therefore is concerned with the design of the physical plant: location, buildings, grounds, and related items for motels. The term design is used, rather than architecture or style, because it has much broader implications. Under this label we can group all those aspects of the physical plant having to do with aesthetic appeal, durability, or functional arrangement. And this broader aspect of motels has much more to do with their attracting and holding customers.

CHAPTER 8

Location and
Site Selection

So often it is said "location is the most significant factor for motel success," and yet how seldom are clear statements made on this topic. In the past, emphasis has been placed upon such rules-of-thumb as: right hand side of road; where there is a great amount of traffic; where most people enter town (not the far side); wherever land is cheap; or away from the noise and congestion of the city. At times there were just enough examples of reasonable success at following such rules that they became axioms. However, as newer and even more successful motels were built in locations which obviously violated these axioms, what went wrong?

Basically, the factor missed in the foregoing fallacies is the guest—his habits and preferences. If we are to judge by those motels he actually patronizes, what can we learn about his needs? To him, for example, whatever is the right hand side coming in becomes the left hand side leaving the community and many new visitors to the community prefer to get through town to expedite the next morning's travel. Modern divided highways further reduce the significance of right or left and force the traveler to be more concerned about signs, exits, and ramps. Volumes of traffic going by the door of a motel are of little real significance except in a very relative way. The authors recall an instance of over 95 per cent occupancy the year around in a motel on a highway with less than 3,000 cars a day (annual average) compared to another which never succeeded with less than 60 per cent occupancy for a three-month

A

Here, a major vacation attraction, Jasper National Park, provides the location logic for successful operation of the Andrew Motor Lodge, Jasper, Alberta, Canada. *Blakey, Blakey, & Ascher, architects.*

B

A pace-setter of the in-town motel concept, the "Motelized" Hotel Mead, Wisconsin Rapids, is as fresh and satisfying (and successful) today as when first built in 1951. *Donn Hougen, architect.*

C

Nearness to the business section and the University of Colorado are significant location factors in the success of the Harvest House, Boulder.

A

Boating, swimming, water-skiing, and other year around water and land-based fun were the chief concern in locating this inn at the Paris Landing State Park, Buchanan, Tennessee. *Clark and Stoll, architects; landscape designers, Mario and Seta.*

Resort-type appeal as well as nearness to community were considered in locating the Doctor's Motel, St. Petersburg, Florida. *Kivett, Meyers, and McCallum, architects.*

One of the greatest man-made attractions of the world, Disneyland
(background), became the major reason for the location of the Disneyland Hotel (foreground), Anaheim, California.

season on a highway with over 13,000 cars a day! Yet both had comparable facilities and management. The significant point here is that people in motion are not necessarily paying guests—they must come to a halt before they are potential occupants. And they are not intending to stop only because a motel has been built there.

What about locations where land is cheap, away from the noises and congestion of the city? For some other use, perhaps, but not for most motels. Cheap land often becomes costly land when computed on the basis of the financial returns. And people may say that they like peaceful and secluded locations but experience demonstrates otherwise when they actually use motels.

So, what do seem to be principles of modern motel location, based upon the guest and his maintenance of high occupancy? Suggested here are five:

1. Nearness to travel objectives
2. Nearness to community services
3. Ease of access
4. Economically suitable land
5. Suitable site characteristics

NEARNESS TO TRAVEL OBJECTIVES

A strong force in motel location is the business or pleasure objective of the guest. For example, a great many salesmen, vendors, business executives may be attracted to a community because of a certain large manufacturing plant or a grouping of several industries. If other conditions are desirable, this favors a location toward these industries. Perhaps a large clinical hospital has developed a state-wide or national reputation and attracts many visitors at all times of the year. A university or large religious center may be the focal point for many overnight guests. Investigation (see Chapter 2) can reveal the relative number of people coming to the area for these various reasons. Perhaps some locations are especially suitable because they serve more than one of these generators of trade.

NEARNESS TO COMMUNITY SERVICES

All travelers wish to reduce the number of interruptions in travel as much as possible and therefore group their stops. The stop for the noon meal is combined with a business appointment. The stop for gas is combined with a coffee break. The stop for the evening meal is also the stop for lodging and entertainment. Somewhere during the travel, purchases of cigarettes, drugs, or camera film may be desired. Sometimes the services of a car mechanic, laundry, or dry cleaning establishment are desired along with a night's lodging.

All these favor the community, rather than a rural or remote setting. This is true of both tourist and business travel. Tourists will, however, tend to favor the suburbs, where there is some open space and yet near community services. The businessman may be attracted to either the city center or the suburbs, depending upon his travel needs that particular night. In any case, the variety of food service businesses, bars, entertainment, drug stores, department stores, car servicing, and the host of services offered by a community are in demand by most travelers. Even in remote resort areas, one finds the greatest potential for overnight accommodations near community locations.

For most communities, two locations seem to be favored today over many others: at a major interchange with main highway and street leading to community (or road leading to major resort area, provided that community services are available nearby); and near the downtown or suburban business and cultural section.

EASE OF ACCESS

No matter how strong the pulling power of certain areas of the community for overnight business, the ease of getting to the location must be considered. Cities now, as never before, are undergoing changes in highways, streets, and the downtown core. Streets which yesterday carried two-way traffic are now one-way; streets which once led out of town lead nowhere; and former minor streets now are important feeders to interchanges, new industries, or new business.

Knowledge of street and highway changes therefore is valuable for estimating the stability of a certain proposed motel location. If routing from main travel objectives is difficult and regulations prohibit ample sign identification, the location may be unsuited to a motel business just because of difficulty of finding it.

ECONOMICALLY SUITABLE LAND

Often prospective motel owners become enamoured over a "real deal" on property, citing low land cost as one of the requisites to their success in the motel business. Sometimes a proposed site is so costly that it is way out of proportion to its potential return. Real estate experts often caution the homeowner about overbuilding in a modest neighborhood. This bit of elementary land economics has much to do with selecting a motel location.

Experience has shown that a desirable range of raw land to the total investment cost is from 10 per cent to 15 per cent for the new motel. In other words, a prospective owner can afford to pay from $20,000 to $30,000 for land if his completed project will cost about $200,000. This is no hard rule and has been violated when other factors dictate change. Sometimes larger land holdings seem desirable because of other anticipated businesses, such as a bowling alley or shops, but in all fairness to the motel, only that portion of land essential to the motel should be considered in estimating land costs.

This approach should suggest that if the raw land cost is very much lower or higher than the limits proposed, it may be better suited to some other business or land use.

SUITABLE SITE CHARACTERISTICS

In selecting the specific site within a general location, the main considerations are size and land quality.

The greatest limitation imposed by the site size is upon parking. Since costs usually dictate on-grade parking, this becomes a veritable land hog. The next biggest land user, of course, is the building itself. Even before purchasing the site, rough estimates of these square footages can be made. A third important aspect of size is land for suitable setting and outdoor recreational development. So much of the success of the total enterprise is dependent upon this factor that such land areas must not be neglected.

Land varies greatly in its characteristics and suitability to motel use. Further details on making a site analysis appear in Chapter 11. Generally, these variations include outside influences upon the site; physical characteristics; climate; legal controls; and visual characteristics.

While detailed site analysis often does not come until after purchase, even brief inspection can demonstrate general suitability to motel use.

In summary, selection of the right location, then, involves skill, knowledge, and fortunate judgement on motel management, traffic, circulation, business generators, real estate, and building planning, just to name a few of the more important items.

CHAPTER 9

The Meaning of Design

Wrapped up in such comments as "I like so-and-so's motel; it is a wonderful place to stay," are favorable impressions of the physical environment as well as good service. The visual impact of the exterior; the impression made upon entering the motel; and of course the satisfying appeal and success of the room design—all are contained in such remarks from satisfied guests.

But, for each reader, his image of *well-designed* facilities may differ slightly or greatly from all others. Therefore, if we are to learn more about this significant phase of motels, we must make more precise delineation of what the abstraction "design" really means to us.

To the tourist, the sweeping drive through a spacious lawn, leading to a one-story wrought-iron porched row of neat room-fronts, may be the ideal. To the salesman, a spacious suite of rooms with provision for displaying his wares and entertaining customers is his picture of the ideal motel. The pink-and-rose room with rich but sensitive decor may be the image of the honeymooner. The design of a motel thus becomes more specific as one begins to define kinds of *trade*.

Today we hear more and more about the motor inn, the city motel, or the resort motel. Zoning officials and city planners continue to debate the correct zone for motels and their relationships to neighboring properties. Investors in new motels weigh the potential of one site against another in terms of competitive economic advantage. The multi-story downtown motel may seem entirely unrelated in design to its suburban cousin, the highway inn. Design, therefore, becomes more meaningful when *location* is considered.

Then there are those travelers who, night after night, prefer not to make new decisions and would rather choose a chain motel for their overnight's lodging. Presumably, the identical design is a symbol of a standard level of quality which satisfies. Others like the individual approach, not wishing to be stereotyped, and therefore choose an independent motel. So, good motel design can vary depending upon the *management pattern*.

At the outset, then, it must be made eminently clear that there exists no one *best* design for all motels and that the most successful design may well be the one most *different* from all others; not just because it is different, but because it more nearly matches the needs of its special group of guests than any other. The continuous march of time and the resulting changes in society force us into the realization of the need for fresh, new concepts if we are to keep pace with the changing times. Above and beyond certain normative concepts, the element of *innovation* must be recognized if design is to remain viable.

If we are attempting to set down more precise rules of good design we seem to be getting farther from, rather than closer to, our goal. Thus

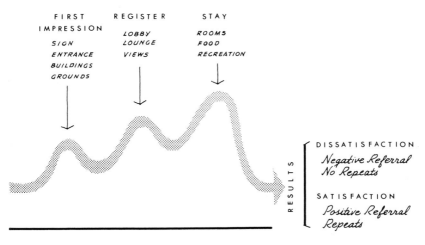

A diagram of the three main peaks of impression motel design and management make upon guests and the consequences of these impressions.

far we have concluded that motel design can vary greatly with the trade, location, or management pattern and should change to keep pace with society as a whole. Is there no common denominator for good motel design? Must every design begin "from scratch" in order to achieve success? A closer look does reveal some measures of motel design which prevail regardless of trade, location, management or point in time. These can be identified as *structural, physical,* and *cultural.*

Will the building withstand severe winds, hail, snow loads, or other forces of nature? Will the materials withstand the wear and tear of use and abuse? Does the structure have the inherent strength to remain in a stable condition for many years? Most of these aspects of the structure today can be subjected to rather precise measurement. Based upon assumptions of stress and strain plus safety factors for the probable exigencies, engineering technology today can provide the answer to most *structural* questions. But merely having a motel that will not fall down or be eaten by termites is not enough. We demand more.

Since we as guests or managers are human beings, our *physical* requirements become very important. Within the building we will be walking, standing, and using a great variety of arm or leg movements. Body similarities and differences become very critical in the design of counters, seats, magazine stands, beds, baths, and elevators. Modern reliance upon mechanical equipment requires an array of controls within reach of maintenance men. Safe drinking water, clean air within desirable limits of comfort are a few of our physical needs. Most of these lend themselves to measurement and some designers have vast files of research information on step ratios, seating heights, and other vital physical data. But are we satisfied with facilities which merely remain erect and allow us to walk, sit, or perform other physical tasks?

What about our psychological recation to the entire facility? Does it express the feeling that inside we will find comfortable and pleasant quarters for our overnight stay? Does the approach to the building present an air of welcome? Does it imply the privacy and security that we desire? Do the dining areas allow us the sociability we want with the group or intimate exclusiveness when dining alone or with a partner? Do we feel that the design matches our social and financial class level? Is it in harmony with the purposes of our trip, such as putting over a big business deal or vacationing with the family? In other words, the design must satisfy a *cultural* need. Measurement of this function is less finite than either mechanical or physical. But, in terms of guest satisfaction, it may even tower above these in importance.

The surrounds and atmosphere are as significant as functional efficiency in food services at motels. South Gate Motor Hotel, Arlington. *Richard Parli, architect.*

A

Another example of a designer's understanding of inside-outside linkage, much appreciated by the guest. *Clark and Stoll, architects; Mario and Seta, landscape designers;* Paris Landing State Park, Buchanan, Tennessee.

B

Cultural design is as much concerned with spatial relationships between buildings as either building or landscape materials. Landscape details by *Edward L. Daugherty, landscape architect* for the Atlanta Hilton Inn, Atlanta, Georgia; *George Sanders, architect.*

C

A   In addition to the aim of a beautiful interior court, *landscape architect Edward Daugherty* here demonstrates the use of design and materials which will require little upkeep. Atlanta Hilton Inn, Atlanta, Georgia; *George Sanders, architect.*

B

Scattered shade and architectural softening tastefully break up a serviceable walk area beside motel parking. *Martini and Associates, landscape architects;* Heart of Atlanta Motel, Atlanta.

The dominance of water recreation often dictates close linkage between guest rooms and the waterscape. *Newton Wilde, interior designer;* Lakeway Inn and Marina, Lake Travis, Austin, Texas.

Lighting of landscape features is valuable in adding to night attractiveness of entire facility; increasing walking safety of guests and staff; and adding an element of security — much appreciated but seldom mentioned by the guests.

A

Courtesy of General Electric Corporation.

The detached structures, clean architectural lines, and careful site arrangement provide a feeling of openness and freedom in a relatively compact setting. Charterhouse Motel, Annapolis; *Victor Gruen, architect.*

B

In good design, then, we are striving for vitality as well as durability and logic. While this is true for all design it has special significance to the motel. In fact, the motel is probably the most outstanding architectural expression of American culture today. Here is a special development in answer to the unique needs of a people who are the most car-borne population in the world. (Even the last link in air, train, or steamship travel is by car.)

CHAPTER 10

Who's Involved in Design?

It is one thing to *expect* endurance, convenience, and all the intangibles which satisfy our psyches but it's quite another to *realize* these goals. Readily we think of the architect's preparation of plans and that the entire design task is his and completely under his control. But what about the limitations on design imposed by the shape of the lot; the problem of obtaining certain materials of construction; or the unavailability of the most desirable site? Who are those, in addition to the *designer,* who have an influence on design? There are several whose influence cannot be side-stepped, such as the *money-lender,* the *land negotiator,* the *construction industry,* the *public,* the *owner* and the *manager,* to name the more important ones.

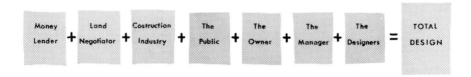

Money Lender + Land Negotiator + Costruction Industry + The Public + The Owner + The Manager + The Designers = TOTAL DESIGN

<hr>

[1]For more complete information on the influences on design, the reader is directed to *Building, U. S. A.* by the editors of Architectural Forum, (McGraw-Hill, 1957) from whom permission was granted for this adaptation.

THE MONEY-LENDER'S INFLUENCE ON DESIGN

Since few motels today are built with cash, the money-lender is a potent force in the majority of new motel developments. His influence can be this great: a decision as to whether or not the motel is to be built. This is worth considering seriously.

Motel construction loans come from a variety of sources but mostly from those primarily money-motivated rather than design-motivated. Decisions are made upon present economic value of land, often dictated by location. Frequently the lender is unfamiliar with motel success in general and puts his faith in the economics of the land rather than the design. Often the decision to loan is based more upon the reputation of the owners and the size of the loan rather than the design.

When this is done, design suffers. Conversely, when the lender is imaginative and far-sighted, he accepts innovation, the very life-blood of good design, and progress is made. Frequently, in the motel business, outstanding designs have been built because the lenders were also part-owners.

States architect, Charles R. Colbert, ". . . poor design, poor invest-ment, and poor patronage are directly connected. While I do not usually blame motel owners and managers, I do condemn the entrepreneurial process which actually demands shoddy and poorly thought through de-signs. If serious changes are to be made in our cityscapes, the part played by motels will be most affected in mortgage banking circles."

LAND NEGOTIATORS

Today a hierarchy of land manipulators controls the initial phases of most building projects. This is sometimes, but not always, divided be-tween real estate operators and land subdividers.

The man who subdivides land fixes its size and shape for many years to come. An individual land parcel becomes a fixed entity with complete and precise legal identity. Whether or not this shape, size, or relation-ship with contiguous lands is compatible with motel use most likely did not enter into its creation. When one obtains title to a piece of land he also buys all the land factors which accidentally come along with it—good or bad. The ease of access to the site; the relation to utilities; the aesthetics of the surroundings—as well as the soil characteristics, topography, and visual appeal of the site itself—all accompany the pur-chase. These, in turn, can dictate the nature of the building design and layout to considerable extent. They may force long rectangularity or boxy squareness. They may force multistory construction when more horizontal design might be more desirable. They may demand open first story for parking, leaving the building on stilts. Yes, the land subdivider does greatly influence motel design and yet motelism is not generally a part of his curriculum.

Today's realtor is far ahead of his predecessors in recognizing some of the art of building. Demands upon his interest, however, are usually greatest from speculative sales rather than design. The short run gain is more readily convertible to cash. Notable exceptions, however, are those real estate developers who have some understanding of design as well as the motel business. Through several land maneuvers, the right grouping of lands is brought together for motel use and a favorable setting for good motel design is created.

THE CONSTRUCTION INDUSTRY

Never underestimate the power of the contractor, his labor force, or the supply of manufactured materials and equipment. Plans are worthless unless interpreted in actual construction and the contractor's influence on making dreams into realities cannot be taken lightly.

Your contractor is virtually the controller of costs. You know nothing about the amount of loan needed until total costs are determined. You can have no knowledge of the estimated financial success of the motel until you know costs of construction and furnishing. Even though your architect has a reputation of offering accurate cost estimates, the precise cost figures will not be secured until fixed bids by contractors are made —and even then some variation can happen between bidding and the completed job. As with the lender, the contractor may very well dictate whether or not the motel is to be forgotten or actually built.

As contractors become more professional, both architects and owners rely upon them more for advice on materials and methods of assembly. How well the dream of the designer is carried out depends greatly upon the skill and interest of the contractor.

His task is not an easy one compared to an assembly-line manufacturing plant. His materials market is much more complicated. From day to day, shifts of price or availability can upset his estimates of total building cost or scheduling, which was part of his risk when making his bid. This influences costs. The great variety of sources of materials also confuses his problem. His labor is difficult to predict. Sometimes as many as 15 different trades may be operating on a job at the same time. Coordination of this labor force is a major undertaking. And how well he does interpret the plan ideas of the designer depends much upon the clarity of the blueprints and specifications and the attitude of the contractor toward the architect and owner.

A word about the manufacturer. The manufacturer of materials which go into buildings is much different from the one supplying an automobile or appliance manufacturer. For one thing, buildings usually constitute but a fraction of his outlet. Building construction takes only 16 per cent of the steel output and only 10 per cent of the glass output, in spite of our present "glass-age" architecture. Manufacturers therefore do not put the interest or research effort into buildings that they demonstrate in other uses of their products. Other aspects of buildings, such as being site-oriented in assembly, individuality of each project, and the aesthetics of buildings tend to dilute his interest in building projects. Even so, the manufacturer is becoming a much more vital force in building design as we lean more heavily upon his products for supply rather than natural materials.

THE PUBLIC

Nor can we ignore the general public in motel design. Their influence is directed in two ways: public taste and legal controls.

At any point in time, public opinion of architectural design is very powerful—good or bad. If one is to judge by what he sees along any established highway approaching the city, the mass taste in building design must be bad. Otherwise, why is there so much ugliness, deformity, and shabbiness in what we see? And motels are no exception.

This was not always so. Back in the handicraft days, design was intimate and personal. Each individual cared greatly about the appearance of things. He was a part of the success or failure of the designs about him and, therefore, strove to polish and perfect his surrounds.

The industrial revolution gave us an opportunity of mass-producing ugliness and our new culture detaches us from design. This is all the more reason for us to be concerned with good design and work harder for its accomplishment. This approach is defensible not only by better business but by its greater contribution to the culture of the community.

No motel owner gets far in his project without having to recognize the power of legal control over his design. Although zoning ordinances and building codes are purported to be founded in health, safety, and welfare, they are potent forces delimiting design. Building setbacks, limits of access, and controls over use often contort design. Architects sometimes feel that little is left for them in the hope of creating a satisfactory solution when hedged in by a multiplicity of legal limitations. These can become costly and time-consuming. For example, the Hilton Hotel designed for San Francisco was held up for a year, at a cost to the firm of $1 million, due to 141 arguments over building restrictions.[2]

The public, then, has much to do with the design of a new motel.

OWNER'S INFLUENCE

Few people hold greater control over design than the owner himself. He is the sole initiator of the project. He prescribes the quantity, quality, and type of business he anticipates, hence, the size of buildings. He makes much, or little, of his obligation to the community. And he resists, or encourages, innovations in design.

But who is the owner? Sometimes an individual, but more likely a group, has the power of decision: a board of directors, syndicate, or partners. The decision to initiate the project, buy the land, and pay for construction is the owner's even though this role is sometimes played by a lender, an architect, or a manager. No matter, the decision to proceed or quit usually rests with the owner—and decisions on *what* will be built are also his. This greatly influences design.

When a person says that he intends to build a "really posh facility" or a "modest family motel," he fixes many design implications before the designer enters the picture. The chain of decisions, beginning with location, site selection, arrangement, and building design, follows directly on the heels of the owner's initial concept of his trade. Most often, he sets the pattern of anticipated volume and level of trade.

His contribution to the community or society as a whole is often limited, however, because of his self-profit orientation. The cultural importance of today's motel in the community is significant especially now that urban locations are being sought. How well the design fits its surrounds; how well its access is coordinated with adjacent businesses; and how its development fits the over-all transportation problem of the community are as much the obligation of the motel owner as the city planner. Encouraging is the general growth of concern over the city scene and the businessman's part in improvement. A large and successful pharmaceutical company states, "all business, large or small, is a part of its community, its state, its nation . . .business must make its contribution to the convenience, beauty, and healthfulness of the community in which it operates."

---

[2]See Architectural Forum, 1961, November.

More than this, the owner has great power over the extent of *innovation* in design. Generally, he is so tightly oriented to balance sheets, business deals, and literal efficiency that he favors the known, the experienced, and therefore, the past. He often asks the designer the question, "Has this been done before?" New and fresh approaches are thus squelched at the start and the past, good or bad, is again repeated. Experience is a good teacher provided that we do learn—learn that some things can be done better.

The story of America is not one of stagnation. The innovator put the nation on wheels and into the air. The innovator brought the bathroom inside the tourist cabin of the depression era. The innovator showed the value of better beds, carpeted floors, and TV in rooms. But these have been on the drawing boards for years—it took owners to put them into effect. The designers generally are not lacking in ideas but it takes decision-makers to put them into effect. The stifling of new ideas appears to be a problem of all business today, according to an astute and progressive manufacturer who names three inhibitors of innovation in all modern business: 1) a modern-day cultural distaste for anything new—fear of upsetting existing norms; 2) cliques of elite in power who filter out nearly all innovations by virtue of their monopoly control; and 3) failure to utilize the creative power normally found in most individuals.[3]

It would seem that a business as sensitive to new needs and desires of people as the motel business warrants the most progressive designs that can be conceived. With society changing more rapidly than ever before, it would seem downright essential that one keep pace with design progress as well as improved interest rates or sale-lease-back financing.

THE MANAGER

Sometimes a forgotten man in design is the manager of a motel. He, among all others, is closest to the life processes of motel operation. A manager brings *experience* to the design. He has seen many things work for him and others fail. He has had close contact with the guests. In a new plan, he can mentally trace the steps of new guests and staff—thereby spotting areas needing revision. His task will be to make the plan work after it is completed; hence, he has a strong incentive to make it efficient and workable. If his experience has taught him insight into people's wants and desires, his advice can be valuable.

---

[3]From "The Management of Innovation," by William T. Brady, president, Corn Products Company, N. Y. in *Business Topics*, E. Lansing, M.S.U., Spring '61, Vol. 9, No. 2.

His experience also can get in his way. The limitations of a single experience may make it difficult for him to imagine the situation at a *new* location, *new* site, and with *new* facilities. His concern over operational activities may dull his imagination and cause general negativism toward all innovation in design.

Even so, it is a mistake to leave the manager out of the earliest discussions of a new motel plan. If the prospective manager is not yet known, all planning should wait until such a person has been named.

THE PROFESSIONAL DESIGNERS

We have purposely saved until last the group of specialists who are obviously concerned with design in order to give the reader an introduction to other and less well-known influences on motel design. By designers we mean all those who bring high skill and professionalism to the project, including architects, interior designers, engineers, landscape architects, sculptors, and other artists.

Ideally, the "design team" approach is the best one. By design team approach we mean close cooperative design made by such professionals as an architect, landscape architect, engineer, interior designer and such other specialists as required by the nature of the design. Seldom is this ideal accomplished, however. Probably the reason is the lack of stimulation on the part of owners. Few prospective owners of motels today realize the potential of this approach. Part of this stems from the fear of unnecessary or overlapping fees. If more professional people are involved in the design, the costs of design may increase. But the increase may be worth it. What difference does it make if some additional dollars are spent on the design process if the result is more outstanding, more functional, and thereby brings greater financial returns? This interrelationship is well spelled out by architect Robert D. Hanson, (Patch and Erickson, Architects): "To be successful architecturally, any business venture involving architecture or any other art or science must also be successful commercially. If it is not, the business dies; and possibly the architecture along with it.

"To accomplish this success, the project must pick up where the advertising (i.e. billboards, etc.) leaves off. It must sell itself upon actual exposure to the potential customer. The project must therefore, offer something of intrigue and delight to appeal to either the person who is accustomed to this sort of thing, or to the majority of us, something which he is not ordinarily accustomed to. In short, a motel should have the quality of design which the connoisseur expects and the masses covet."

The days of planning motels by staying in a few and giving a building contractor some pencil scratches on a napkin or back of an envelope are gone. Today's motel demands careful, skillful, and thoughtful designing by those who know all facets of motel design. While no one can deny that some highly successful motels today were designed by nonprofessionals, the logic of this cannot be reversed to say that all motels should be designed this way. A person may survive a knife-cut by application of simple home first aid, but more than one person has been kept from losing a hand or arm through more complete diagnosis and treatment by a professional physician. Nor is this to say that professional men never make mistakes. At least, the probabilities are in our favor of having better results from those who have had special training, talent, and experience in either medicine or design.

The best design should come from the team approach, but too seldom is the entire team around to hear the opening gun. No matter who is at fault, this is unfortunate. The engineer might have been able to offer vital cost-saving suggestions if he had been called in earlier. The landscape architect, a specialist in site selection and arrangement, can do little more than "posey planting" if called in too late. A food service specialist can do little to improve the efficiency of kitchen layout if decisions on doors and utilities are already fixed. This is one of the complications of modern specialization and we pay for it dearly. We pay for it with too many revisions of plans. We pay for it with added costs of construction. We pay for it with inefficiencies of building use after construction. Above all, we pay for it in design sacrifices—architectural failures and emotional failures. And many would stand firm on the premise that architectural failures are destined to be business failures.

Let's look at the influence of these specialists on design.

Engineers have replaced the outdoor biffy with the gleaming, white porcelain jobs; the pot-bellied stove with thermostats and radiant heat; hazardous grade intersections with bridges and underpasses. A multitude of improvements in our daily living can be attributed to the engineer. The main difference between the tavern of 1835 and the motel of today is largely in the comforts and conveniences developed by the engineers.

But sometimes their brilliance and technology carries them too far, too fast. The face of the earth can be changed in a twinkling of an eye by modern earth-moving practices—much to the alarm of nature lovers and conservationists. New, well-engineered highways ruthlessly uncoil their concrete tentacles through farms and forests in a hasty effort to improve point-to-point transportation—but ignore human values, such as landscape

beauty, along the way. Electronic robots maintain fine adjustments on motel heating boilers—but engineering hyperspecialization often ignores other factors contributing to guest comfort, such as sound or humidity control. To the engineer we are deeply indebted. His concentrated specialization has cut deeply into our ignorance and helplessness, sometimes so deeply that no one sees over the ridges thus formed.

Up to this point, we have not deliberately wished to strip the *architect* of any glory, but perhaps have demonstrated that *all* design is not of his making—others influence it greatly. Our main point here is that when these many other influences are recognized, much more intelligent designing can take place and the function of the architect becomes more clear.

The popular concept of the architect is that of plan-drawer. While this part of the design process is a significant function of his office, we are doing him a disservice if this is all we want or expect of him. Blueprints and specifications are the traditional documents prepared by architects to convey their picture of the completed project to the client and builder. The significance lies in the creativity, originality, and brilliance of problem-solving rather than in the lines and words in these documents, essential as they are. Without the architect, we have only buildings—not architecture. The repetition of stale, monotonous, and unimaginative motels throughout the country is mute testimony to the dearth of motel architecture—only a multiplicity of motel buildings. Perhaps the greatest contribution of the architect is his ability to incorporate feeling, emotion, and that elusive original sparkle into otherwise strictly utilitarian structures. The expedient, the practical, the utilitarian, however, sometimes even dampen his ability to perform his greatest role—design creativity. Owners and managers are particularly prone to ignorance or disinterest in this aspect, making the architect the sole defender of progress in architecture. Recent interest in new motel design

An example of sensitivity to site, allowing the beautifully tree-covered setting to dominate the entire design concept of this motel is pictured at left. The undulating topography and the dramatic tree sculptures would have been destroyed with the typical motel layout. The site plan and further photographs of the motel are shown on pages 64 and 65. The Mark Thomas Inn, Monterey, California, designed by John Carl Warnecke and Associates, architects; Lawrence Halprin, landscape architect.

The coarse-textured informality of the plant materials offers an appropriate base for the massive oak and the rough-textured warmth of the motel building itself.

A   The power of the landscape setting is interrupted only slightly by the use of separate, relatively small but feasible motel building units.

As one approaches the units more closely, the simple yet neat and trim lines of the landscape and pool spell out superior comfort and cleanliness to the guest and yet retain the back-to-nature, rustic setting.

B

After the transition to the interior is made, a traveler is welcomed by this inviting lounge, spotlighted by the skylights.

C

High, picturesque trees outside are repeated in the high ceiling, window screen, and indoor plants of the dining room which face into the motel court.

Site plan, designed by *Lawrence Halprin, landscape architect.*

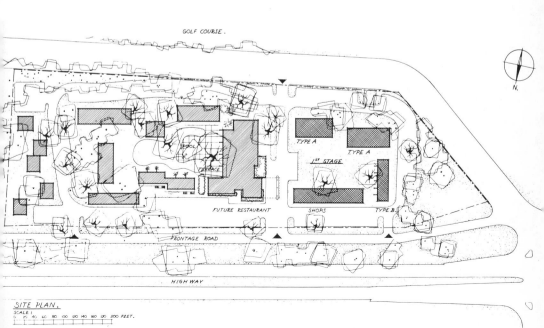

GOLF COURSE.

N.

POOL

TERRACE

TYPE A

TYPE A

1ST STAGE

FUTURE RESTAURANT

SHOPS

TYPE B.

FRONTAGE ROAD

HIGHWAY

SITE PLAN.
SCALE :
0 20 40 60 80 100 120 140 160 180 200 FEET.

approaches, such as the Islandia Hotel and Restaurant, San Diego, is refreshing evidence of improved attitude on this score.

The architect often assumes the role of leader-coordinator in the total design. Special functional aspects of a motel-design job may require 10, 15 or 20 specialists, ranging from pool designers to sign artists. It is difficult for a client (owner) to negotiate with so many individuals and certainly he should not have the responsibility for coordination of their specialties. By placing this task in the hands of the building or landscape architect, the process of design should work more smoothly, the building and its setting should have design harmony, and the mechanics of contractural agreements should be much simplified.

More and more, those who concentrate upon the detailing of building interiors, *interior designers,* consider themselves in a special profession even though the role is often performed by architects and merchants of interior furnishings. Regardless of who does the work, the interiors of all motel spaces deserve the highest quality of design creativity. These designers should have such objectives in mind as an up-to-date first impression upon new guests; warm, hospitable, convenient, and comfortable quarters to build repeat business; an eye to upkeep and maintenance along with visual appeal and close integration with the over-all architectural expression for the intended clientele. This cannot be done by flashing every new fad before the public nor by pursuing only a decorating or fancying process. Some observers of design have made the sage comment that the best interior design is that in which the physical room goes unnoticed but in which the people take on prime importance.

A study of motel-like development in a man-made resort setting, the Islandia Hotel and Restaurant are the first parts of a funland development, 4,600-acre Mission Bay Aquatic Park, San Diego, whose over-all concept was the creation of a design team: Simon Eisner, city planner; Smith and Williams, architects; and Eckbo, Dean and Williams, landscape architects.

The motel and restaurant are the result of further team effort: Eugene Weston III, Eugene Weston, Jr., and Frederick Liebhardt, architects; landscape design by Harriet Warner and Joseph Yamada; LaJolla Interiors, William Short, interiors. Additional photographs appear on pages following. Photos courtesy of California Redwood Association.

A   Proof that motels need not be of monotonous, stereotyped, or traditional architecture is the front view of the Islandia Hotel. The decorative hat-forms conceal sky-ways, offering light and ventilation to a semienclosed corridor below.

Detail of sky-way opening onto semienclosed corridor serving all rooms. This unique solution provides the functional efficiency of an interior corridor and yet captures some of the freedom associated with typical outdoor access.

Here, the open landscape demanded careful attention to all phases of both site and buildings. Dominant use of redwood blends walls, roofs, walks, entrances, and buildings together. Note restaurant buildings of harmonious yet slightly different design.

A

Closer view of restaurant shows how generous use of wood (entrance, border, railing, building exterior), together with integrated design, links restaurant with motel and parking.

B

A seven-hexagon restaurant building completely surrounded by water maximizes views. Evidence of design skill is shown here in blending exterior with interior. The inside becomes a part of the outdoors and yet provides the sense of protection and enclosure of an indoor area.

A

Striped floors and walls are relieved by the plain, smooth textured bedspreads, crisp furnishings, and decorative tapestries.

B

Detail of cocktail lounge peak with light cluster.

C

Interior designers, no matter how they perform their tasks, have a significant influence upon that elusive but vital aspect of all motel business: guest satisfaction. Through their concern over the artistic as well as the utilitarian, they can create satisfying interiors with their colors, lighting, furnishings, and room arrangement. But, to be most successful, their efforts must be intimately tied in with the other specialists of design.

Site development, site planning, or landscape architecture—no matter what you call it, is the design contribution which can be made by the *landscape architect.* As with building interiors, the design of the space-beyond-the-building has much to do with the business success of the entire establishment. The guest's first impression obtains from a complete visual sweep of building, sign, grounds, trees, and surrounding neighborhood. To the guest, it is one whole. The landscape therefore cannot be treated in isolation, which is often done by those having little understanding or only special interest in plant material. Improper placement of trees and other plants; poor siting of entrance; difficult automobile circulation; and visual delimitation of the building architecture are a few of the negative results from efforts of the untrained and inexperienced. Packing a site with expensive evergreens or using extensive park design principles are not in the interest of either the management or the clientele.

Because site development and successful landscape result from the proper composition of all elements of the site, the landscape architect must be brought in early if he is to perform his best service. With the other design specialists, the assets of the site can be magnified, the liabilities minimized, and new developments added to provide the ultimate in beauty as well as utility. While this may appear to be more significant in the resort where the land takes on greater volume of interest it is beginning to be recognized as important in the cityscape. Implicit in modern urban renewal, which includes city motel sites, is site design of high harmony with all other redevelopment.

A rare man in the design team is the *sculptor* or *mural artist.* He complains of relegation to a purely decorative chore, and then only after all major design decisions have been made. This seems a strange paradox in motel design inasmuch as visual impression and atmosphere are held to be great elements of promotion in the minds of business management experts.

The complexities of modern building have forced specialization in design to an almost unworkable degree, yet the demand for the results

Deep overhang allows sun shield and protection of board walk. Room recesses provide privacy when desired. Note simple, effective, and coordinated design of light fixtures.

A

This end view demonstrates the careful consciousness of scale bringing a relatively large building into close harmony with the site and completely within the grasp of all who approach it.

B

of such specialization continues to increase. It therefore is difficult for a motel to be built today without bringing in a television specialist, a swimming pool designer, and an expert in electronic equipment for intercom and room control. If a restaurant is contemplated, specialists in kitchen layout, equipment selection, and dining room interiors are also sought. It is not unlikely that a sign artist and an outdoor lighting specialist will also be utilized. In almost all of his design work, the architect calls in structural engineers, electrical engineers, and mechanical engineers as a matter of course.

Perhaps it can be seen by now that the owner's first idea of his motel is pounded, hammered, and shaped by quite an army of influential individuals (few of whom are designers) before it takes on its final form of construction. Reduction of the problem by elimination of a specialist here or there seems less and less likely. Rather, the hope of the owner in all this is greater coordination and integration so that the final product —a well-designed environment for travelers—expresses unity of purpose throughout its design.

CHAPTER 11

The Design Approach

What kind of metamorphosis takes place from the time a motel idea is first conceived to the day of open house? How does one get from the point of land purchase to registering the first guest? What really happens within the activity labeled by the hackneyed phrase, "planning and construction"? There are many routes, some of which arrive very near to the desired goal—others which never quite make it. The process to be discussed here is held out more as a recommendation than fact. It is founded well enough in fact, however, to lend it validity as a recommendation. Few motels, if any, have been completely developed along this pattern, but today's trends favor greater popularity of this approach. Higher investments, narrower profits, and shorter-run enterprise tend to force more careful and precise planning.

Although the page sequence of book presentation forces us to a 1, 2, 3, 4 order, (as identified in diagram,) we would not insist that the design process flow only in this manner. Broadly, point 2 does follow 1 and point 4 does follow 2 and 3, but the flow back from 3 to 2 or 1 must be held open at all times. The diagram is an attempt to illustrate graphically the process which we are expounding. Broadly, the main steps consist of *analysis, synthesis, conceptualization, planning,* and *construction,* but at all times taking full cognizance of *feedback.* The next few pages will be devoted to an explanation of this process.

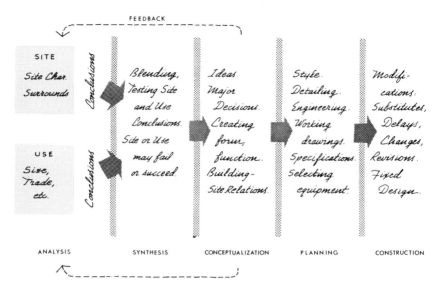

A diagram illustrating a modern theory of the design process, now in practice by some designers. When carried out with a high degree of competence, it assures the ultimate in structural, physical, and cultural design.

ANALYSIS

It is in this first step many building projects fail. Too frequently, a motel design (and therefore the designer) is damned for weaknesses or failures in design, when the facts of the case are that the initial thinking (mostly by others) was wrong or weak.

States architect, Carl Koch: "If another company were to get better design for their chain, they would undoubtedly go ahead of ————— provided they had the other ingredients of aggressive promotion, national advertising, and a relatively high line of service. The hitch is to find commercial entrepreneurs these days who are willing to give a good architect a chance to do this with sufficient time and money for research." A completed design can be little better than the limitations imposed by a poorly selected location or site. The business failure of a luxury design motel cannot be blamed solely on architectural design errors. Without thorough study of both the *site* and the intended *use*, the finished project may be based upon too many unknowns or false assumptions. Even at best, so many unpredictables can happen that it certainly behooves one to eliminate all the guesswork possible.

Site Analysis

Whenever one says "I have purchased this site for a motel," a host of design limitations or opportunities are thus fixed. This is what makes careful site selection so difficult. This is why there is no substitute for thorough site analysis.

OUTSIDE INFLUENCES

Just as our personalities are the product of our environment as well as our own making, thus a specific site must be analyzed in the context of its setting. Many a "beautiful site" has turned out to be a motel failure because of influences outside the site.

Few factors have had greater impact upon both motels and hotels than transportation, yet this factor is often misunderstood. Volume of traffic flow, for example, has far less influence on motel success than most other factors, such as nearness to a potential demand. We sometimes forget that highways provide for *movement* of vehicles, not stoppage; and snaring rapidly moving vehicles has proven to be quite a feat, not only by the space explorer but the motel operator. Better highways do *provide* for greater volume of traffic, but how much of that traffic, by its own decision, chooses to be near our site and how well it has access to our site are significant considerations.

Although automobile transportation dominates the field, plane, ship, bus and rail travel should not be discounted. For specific types of trade, these travel systems can exert a greater influence on a specific site. *Airtels* and *boatels* are not flighty expressions of some promoter's scheme but an honest reaction to definite travelers' needs. Certainly a modern airport is not the quietest place on earth and privacy is at a premium. However, successful operations at such points have proven the point that some travelers are either attracted to the display of air traffic or have all their travel objectives within close range of the terminal, and prefer to stay close to their arrival and departure points. Analysis might reveal the need for overnight accommodations in connection with harbors and ports, considering the boom in boating and water recreation.

Following these broader measures of outside influences, what about those influences immediately outside the property? Each and every land use on the neighboring properties should be identified and considered in light of its possible effect upon motel business. Are these uses about to change—either through natural growth or legal control, such as zoning? What is the nature of the topography, particularly with regard to drainage patterns? Would any adjacent use be considered a sound, odor, visual or other nuisance? What approaches to the property can be obtained?

By now it may be clear that no site can be considered in isolation. What potentialities it may have as a motel site derive as much from its surroundings as from within the property boundary.

Site Characteristics

Inherent within every site are characteristics which limit or support motel development. Foreknowledge of these is essential if costly errors are to be avoided.

Accurate knowledge of the topography is essential. This is necessary for the designer in determining whether the contours might best remain as they are or should be altered in some way. Changes in land elevation have a direct bearing on the visual appeal of a completed project. Worthwhile vistas may be obtained or precluded by the degree of understanding the lay of the land. The provision for rain-water runoff, snow removal, and the permanent siting of the buildings can be made properly only when complete topographic knowledge of the land is available.

The amount and nature of the vegetative cover should be studied. Whether a complete forest or a single tree, the existing plant materials should be noted and well understood and may set the theme for the development of the site.

Soil studies are necessary to know the bearing strength for building support and suitability to drives, parking, and other construction as well as plant growth where desired. Rock underlayment or outcrop may be an asset or a liability—but should be known.

Knowledge of the over-all as well as the microclimate of the site contributes to the complete understanding of the motel project and its environment. Rainstorms, snowfall, hail or winds can be rather troublesome and even destructive. Their frequency and severity should be considered in the design.

An important part of any site analysis is knowledge of legal controls over the site. How do the building codes, zoning ordinances and deed restrictions limit or control development? Is the property affected by easements or rights-of-way? Is there a city or regional planning body; if so, what is their belief of the future of this site?

Here have been suggested just some of the items a site analysis could bring to the attention of the designer and owner. In any case, the more that is known beforehand, the more likely will be the design—and business—success.

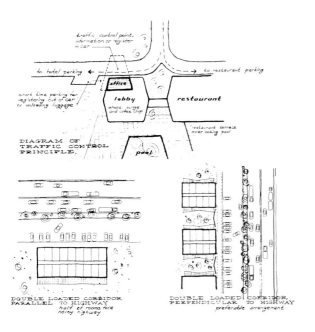

traffic control point.
information or register
in car

to hotel parking ←   → to restaurant parking

office

short time parking for
registering out of car
or unloading luggage

lobby
shops, lounge
and coffee shop

restaurant

restaurant terrace
overlooking pool

DIAGRAM OF
TRAFFIC CONTROL
PRINCIPLE.

pool

DOUBLE LOADED CORRIDOR
PARALLEL TO HIGHWAY
half of rooms face
noisy highway

DOUBLE LOADED CORRIDOR
PERPENDICULAR TO HIGHWAY
preferable arrangement

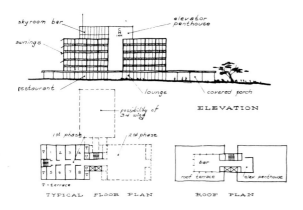

skyroom bar   elevator
                               penthouse

awnings

restaurant   lounge   covered porch

ELEVATION

possibility of
3rd wing

1st phase   2nd phase

bar

roof terrace   elev. penthouse

T · terrace

TYPICAL FLOOR PLAN   ROOF PLAN

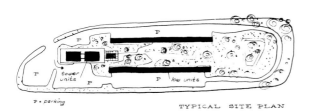

tower
units

low units

P = parking

TYPICAL SITE PLAN

Typical site and building studies — for Charterhouse Inns as prepared by *Victor Gruen, Associates, architects*, for the Hotel Corporation of America. These illustrate some of the functional considerations of use and adaptation to site.

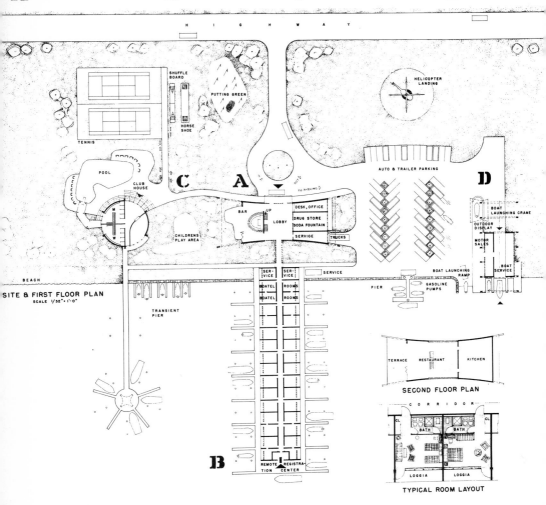

A CENTRAL BUILDING   **B** LIVING UNIT   **C** RECREATION   **D** SERVICE

Site development and architectural study for a *boatel*, prepared by *Pavlecic and Kovacevic, architects,* for the Scott-Atwater organization. This reflects the modern trend of providing for many services at one site rather than the traditional approach of lodging or food service only. With suitable climatic conditions and location factors, occupancies could be sufficient for business success.

A   Because of their high cost, models should be reserved for final design stage uses such as demonstration of special building-site relationships or project promotion. Early analysis and first concepts must be kept fluid, requiring more flexible methods of graphic representation. The *boatel* by *Pavlecic and Kovacevic.*

A typical rendering of a proposed project to illustrate to the owner, manager, and investors just how the buildings and site would appear when completed. Prospective owners, however, should not push for such renderings until the architects have completed their research on both site and use analyses and developed basic concepts for the major design problems. Charterhouse Motor Lodge, Annapolis; *Victor Gruen, architect.*

B

CHARTERHOUSE MOTOR LODGE

Annapolis, Maryland

The authors' commentary on a typical downtown motel site development and plan.

1. The identifying sign must be easily read from both directions and can be a part of the building design.

2. Site conditions may dictate a loop or single drive entrance, which is usually acceptable because of slowed traffic.

3. The entrance canopy, reminiscent of the carriage stop, is again becoming popular. Leave an open drive for high trucks and cartop carriers.

4. Registration and information desk should be easy to find as one first enters the motel. The front desk area may also include sales of souvenirs, magazines, newspapers, cigars, cigarettes, as well as space for mail and phone calls.

5. A lounge is needed but can be of small size. Plan it as a separate area—not a passageway.

6. An office for correspondence, auditing, bookkeeping, and all record keeping is desirable. In larger motels it should be separate from the manager's private office.

7. A small apartment is desirable for the manager, but most operators prefer their home elsewhere for greater family privacy.

8. A favorable first impression should be created by the exterior design and upkeep.

9. Parking may or may not be visible from the entrance as long as it is reasonably convenient to building entrances.

10. Interior corridor access is acceptable and reduces construction and upkeep costs. A few outside entrances (and stairwells, if more than one story) can offer convenient access to all rooms.

11. Several stories seem to be acceptable. However, over two stories requires an elevator properly located in relation to building entrances, guest rooms, and other public areas.

12. A central storage and control for linens, supplies and cleaning equipment is important. Also provide at least one staff locker room with toilets and lavatories for each sex.

13. A separate room for all electrical control panels, plumbing, heating and air conditioning controls should be centrally located. Another room should be provided for making minor repairs.

14. Some space must be provided for storage of tools, equipment and supplies which must be kept on hand but are not in use most of the time.

15. Dining room, souvenir shop, snack bar, cocktail lounge, barber shop, and other shops are important adjuncts to this business and each one has its own specific requirements for location and planning.

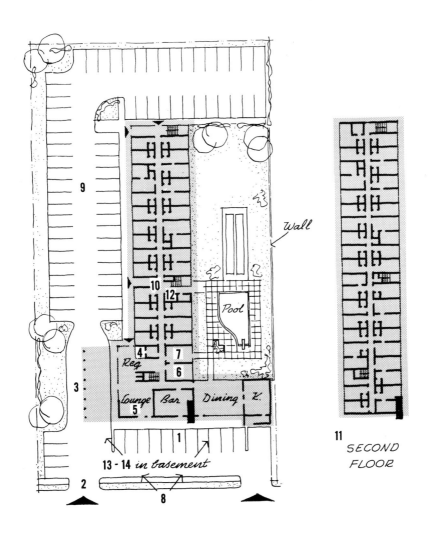

Wall

Pool

Reg

Lounge
5

Bar

Dining

K.

4
7
6
12
10
9
3

1

2

13 - 14 in basement

8

11
SECOND
FLOOR

Suggested development for a motel catering primarily to tourists.

1. The sign should be the first item seen; simple, neat, legible, in keeping with building style.

2. Two entrance drives are preferred; a single drive permissible in slowed traffic zone.

3. Registration desk readily accessible; some use drive-in window. Plan space around desk for guest to get information, register, and buy sundry items. Desk must include equipment ar d records necessary for daily management.

4. A lounge is not essential but many find it desirable, even when small. Can be used as "TV" or "Coffee" room.

5. Private office for manager is desirable to keep records; files; handle private business.

6. Manager's home or apartment with motel is convenient, but makes private family life difficult. In estimating costs and returns, do not figure the home as part of the business investment.

7. Make good first impressions with good layout. Swimming pool, shuffleboard court, appealing grounds and buildings have promotional value.

8. Parking should be laid out for easy use by the guest. Marking is easier when parking is surfaced.

9. Tourists prefer direct access from car to room. They tend to resist interior corridors.

10. Row-type construction is usually preferred, but detached units or duplexes are also used (sometimes dictated by terrain).

11. Place buildings so that best views can be seen from the guest rooms.

12. One story construction preferred; more stories acceptable; but use only when site limitations force building design upward.

13. Build central room for storage and control of linens, cleaning supplies and equipment. At least one locker room with toilet and lavatory should be placed on each floor.

14. Place controls of electrical, heating, plumbing and air conditioning systems in one room easily accessible to the manager. Provide a separate room for tools and equipment for making minor repairs.

15. Consider some area for storage of seasonal and other necessary items. Don't let it become a catchall.

16. Supporting businesses such as food service, car service, and souvenir sales are desirable with the motel or adjacent thereto, but must be planned according to their own factors of success.

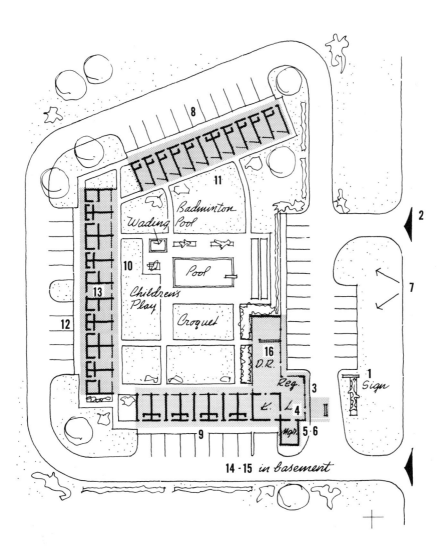

8

11

Badminton
Pool

Wading Pool

10

Pool

Children's
Play

Croquet

13

12

16
D.R.

Reg.

3

1
Sign

4

9

K.

Mgr. 5 6

14 - 15 *in basement*

2

7

Some suggestions on the possible layout and design for a resort type motel on a compact site.

1. The sign on the highway as well as the entrance (sometimes the same) must be simple, legible, designed in harmony with the resort, and given an attractive landscape setting.

2. Either double or single entrance drives are acceptable. Consult your highway department for entrance drive permits and rules on sign set-back, type and lighting.

3. As soon as the guest enters the resort proper, he should find the registration office easily. This office should be located to give the manager complete control of the property.

4. Parking should be of the right size and shape; more than 1 to 1 ratio is desirable. Guests prefer parking near units, but will walk a reasonable distance. Keep view open.

5. Most commonly used play activities (pool, shuffleboard) should be centered to create unity and fellowship among guests. Consider safety when locating horseshoes, archery.

6. Waterfront activities can provide fun for all ages, but must be planned for safety as well. A dock for swimmers and sunbathers should be separated from the boat dock for fishermen. Zones for nonswimmers, beginners, and swimmers should be clearly marked.

7. A screened-in shelter at the waterfront gives parents a chance to relax while supervising children's play. Rainy-day fun can be centered here and the building can provide boat storage in winter.

8. For fishermen, provide a separate dock, launching ramp, lockers for their gear, fish cleaning house, and maybe freezing privileges.

9. All units (detached or in one building) should have view to lake. This takes careful study, considering future construction as well as present needs.

10. Plan for some storage so that it can be enclosed. This can eliminate a tendency in many resorts to have cluttered and unsightly storage areas.

11. A small shop for minor repairs is essential. Hand and power tools and spare parts are needed for the upkeep of the great number of buildings and equipment on the property.

12. Someone in charge must be available at all times. However, some managers prefer to have their own home or apartment elsewhere for greater family privacy.

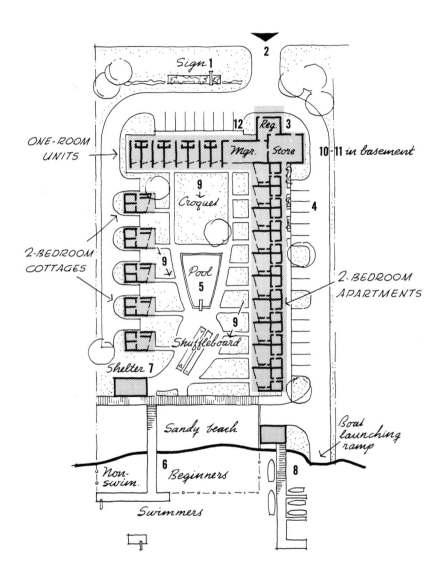

Sign 1

ONE-ROOM
UNITS →

12 Reg 3
Mgr. Store

10-11 in basement

9
↓
Croquet

4

2-BEDROOM
COTTAGES

9
↓

Pool
5

2-BEDROOM
APARTMENTS

9

Shuffleboard

Shelter 7

Boat
launching
ramp

Sandy beach

Non-
swim.

6 Beginners

8

Swimmers

SITE CONCLUSIONS

A site study should give the analyst sufficient data to reach some conclusions about the site. Its main assets and liabilities as well as unusual characteristics are thus made known. The owner, the designer, and all other parties having interest in the motel then have the facts before them.

An example was the case in which an owner had proposed a motel on a site whose location factors seemed to be highly desirable. The land was being used for vegetable production and the soil appeared to be suitable and uniform within the property boundaries. Soil probing, however, revealed varying depths of peat, ranging from 6 inches to 30 feet. Because peat compresses under loads, the construction engineer estimated costs of foundations placed upon piling. This would not have precluded construction of a motel, but the additional cost so favored another location with better site characteristics that the site was abandoned.

It may seem laborious to undertake such a detailed study of a site, but only in this manner can complete understanding of it be accomplished.

Analysis of Use

Clear, complete, and experienced ideas of the type of motel business are as essential to the design of the facilities as site characteristics. Unlike the latter, however, some speculation is required. Who is to say what the business will be like when the facilities are complete? Who can predict what volume or level of trade will be most profitable? Difficult as these may be, someone had better make some educated guesses or you will be paying the designers dearly for extra fumbling on your part.

At this stage in the design process, it is well to regard for a moment the desired uses completely independently from the site. When conclusions regarding use are reached it will be time to play them against the site to test feasibility.

"I think the best building design is that one which really fits the program required by the client. It is a logical outgrowth of the architect translating the particular needs of his client into building spaces. I think that this kind of approach in building design will clearly reflect what is happening inside the building.

"Too many of our recent American architects have been concerned merely with the outer skin and appearance of the building and not in the real space needs of a particular building problem. This is mere 'skin deep architecture' or a superficial styling approach. Many new motels being built in the country have this superficial quality.

"We need to study the functional needs of the building and to create in three dimensions the kind of spaces that will logically meet that need. This kind of approach will bring real meaning to the people who will be using the building. The spaces will actually give a 'particular look' to a building. It is no longer a style but a logical growth of form." So states architect Gyo Obata.

What kind of trade is intended? Modern trends indicate increasing difficulty for any one establishment to satisfy all needs for all people. Variety of trade for a motel is desirable, especially when other factors point to seasonal or other limitations, but the American people today appear to be much more selective than in the past. At present, a great number of motel types are in effect whereas a decade ago a single motel prototype was well understood by all. An example is the Holiday Inn whose original single type has grown into three: The Metropolitan (35 stories in Chicago); The Holiday Inn (prototype); and the Holiday Inn Junior (economy size and price).

Somehow, both the design team and owner should make as complete an estimate of the nature of the prospective business as possible. No architect can be expected to design for an unclear function. Architect Victor Gruen[1] anticipates three general types of motels to emerge from the "almost chaotic confusion of new motel construction: 1) in-town motor hotel; 2) suburban motel hotel; 3) highway lodge." No matter whether everyone agrees with his classification or not, the point is that the nature of the business must be projected before any logical planning or creative design work can begin. Following are some of the items necessary in such a use analysis:

Total number to be housed overnight.
How this number breaks down: families; couples; singles, etc.
Socioeconomic status of clientele: businessmen; executives; service laborers; truckers; conferees; vacationists, etc.
Seasonal estimates of various types of trade.
Degree of luxuries preferred by trade.
Approximate rate to be anticipated.
Number and nature of other services: coffee shop, restaurant, cocktail lounge, souvenir shop, etc.
Per cent of trade coming by automobile; taxi; etc.

---

[1] In July, 1961 issue, *Tourist Court Journal*, Temple, Texas.

Need for conference space

Type of motel administration to be used and its space needs.

Type of housekeeping and maintenance operation; space needs.

A dominant local or business theme and how it might affect the design.

Significance of staging—capacity and type to build for now and what types of expansion are anticipated.

Conclusions Pertaining to Use

The act of preparing the foregoing use analysis has a twofold advantage. It forces the investigation of many possibilities which otherwise might be overlooked. Secondly, because of this analysis, more definite

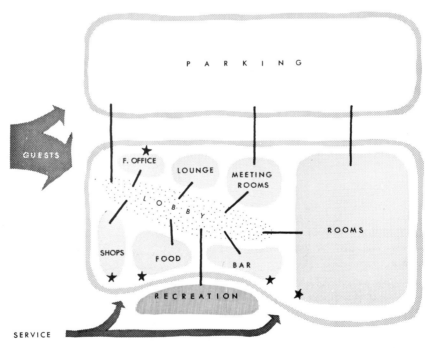

★ *Points of Management Control*

Diagram of basic motel functional relationships. Contrary to a staff organization chart, this suggests logical physical relationship between various functional units.

conclusions can be drawn regarding the intended functional uses—the very foundation for good design.

As a result of using this approach, some prospective motel owners have decided completely against the business. After learning more about the nature of the operation, it seemed less glamorous. Others, who proceeded with their project, have found that their use analysis saved several years of unnecessary and costly experimentation with various types of trade, and therefore they found themselves years ahead of their competitors.

With the results of both the *site analysis* and *use analysis* the design process has made an effective start. However, even yet the art and creativity of design have not come into play. By now, the significance of analysis to both owner and designer may be clear. It is as if one has the tools with which he can proceed with the job—the next step is to bring these two major studies together to see their full meaning.

SYNTHESIS

The next logical step is to bring the results of the use study against the conclusions of the site analysis. When performed objectively, this is quite revealing. When done with prejudice in favor of (or against) either the site or intended use, it means little. This phase, called synthesis, therefore should be done by someone who can look at the entire project with an open mind—and seldom can this be done by the owner alone. With information the owner can supply, this is most effectively done by the members of the design team: architect, landscape architect, etc.

This step should raise questions regarding the suitability of the site. It may even force the all-important decision—whether to proceed with or abandon the project. This step is not yet utilizing design talent or experience in very great degree. It does involve gross planning principles, however. For example, the use analysis may have revealed an optimum number of rooms, which in turn would require a certain amount of parking space. The parking area subtracted from the site area provides a simple statement of the buildable area.

This, then, forces estimates of the number of floors required in the motel or may indicate the need for underground parking or additional land for such use. It is this step which helps the owner understand the limitations or opportunities on his proposed site. So-called plan sketches are not yet necessary except in very rough form. In fact, more helpful are case examples of like-size motels already built upon similar land situations.

CONCEPTUALIZATION

This is the ideational phase—the creative design phase. Here is where so much of motel planning in the past has fallen short. This is the step requiring the many-faceted talents and experiences of all members of the design team. This is the phase few owners can accomplish unless they, by their own right, are also designers.

Up to this point, little if any sketching, drawing, or "designing," in its literal sense, has taken place. Imagination and innovation have not entered the process—only logical and analytical study.

Here, then, is perhaps the most critical step of the entire process— and one most difficult to talk about. Regardless of how impossible to define or understand, it is most vital to design success. We believe in and work around a great many beautiful things we can neither explain nor fully understand, such as the sunrise and the sunset. Such is the nature of design. Here is the step involving that delicate but real balance of a phase of man's activity and his environment for that activity. This is the human step of the design process. It is the one requiring the best from the designer.

Most of us, as children, learned about the great artists and composers who in a dream, by divine decree, or by supernatural power received the inspiration and drive to create beautiful paintings, sculpture, and music. Most of our historic greats in the building arts appear to have had such characteristics of the genius. This indefinable characteristic is argued by some as being 90 per cent perspiration and 10 per cent inspiration but regardless is essential to artistic success. This is not the place to define or expand the virtues of creative art except to emphasize its significance in this type of designed environment—motels.

It is during this phase of the design process that the designer begins to mold a form—to create a new environment. Based upon the factual, functional, and practical, he attempts to form a whole which fulfills the intended purpose. It is here that the trite labels of the artist take on reality. It is here that the designer concerns himself with scale, proportion, texture, color, rhythm and all such elements known to designers. His powers of perception, together with either learned or intuitive art principles, are brought into play for the first time. His knowledge of the human being, his habits, desires, and needs are interpreted in his shaping of a form. He utilizes all the so-called design principles known to the arts, such as balance, sequence, contrast, etc.

Even so, the specifics and details of the design are yet to come. These first attempts at bringing together the creativity of the artist and the logic of specific site and use demands are most productive when only first *concepts* are formed. Several approaches—hence several concepts—of solution may be necessary before the most desirable one is reached. This is a thought process, not one of sheer experimentation. It should be emphasized that this is not the trial-and-error approach sometimes employed by pseudo-designers who believe that the law of probabilities will ultimately give them a workable solution if they make enough trials. Rather, this is a matter of interpreting the factual and logical in several different ways in a desire to arrive at the most complete fulfillment of need—in this case, a designed environment for travelers overnight.

An example is the work of Architect Eldridge Spencer for the National Park Service, who states, "The architect must create an environment that expresses an awareness of the components of the Park, one that recognizes and enhances these without dominating the surroundings. Such an architecture should rest lightly on the soil—it should not compete in scale with the natural components of the park. It should articulate space inside and out, it should provide a practical shelter and protect man from man, but most of all it should give a form of delight. It should be refreshing, not depressing, and it should be temporal in comparison with its timeless setting."[2]

Perhaps by now the reader recognizes the significance of these first vital steps in the design process: that designing a motel is not merely "sketching up a few buildings." By now it may be understood that the future success of the motel as a business is highly contingent upon the amount and quality of thinking in these early stages. It may now be clear that several aspects of motel design precede decisions on wall materials, window sizes, and mechanical systems. Not that these are not important in the final completed design, but that they become even more meaningful if and when a clear concept of the design is formed.

By now it also may be understood that this is a cooperative effort, requiring the time of several talented and experienced people. This costs money. When budgeting costs, the individual therefore should make considerable allowance for these first steps—that is if he wants the best design. Architects, landscape architects, and interior designers continually lament about this aspect of their work. Too many owners want fixed design ideas too fast, forcing the design team to hurdle these first and very important steps. And the results show it. All design fees should be as much a part of the building budget as plumbing labor costs. Good

---

[2]From *Western Architect and Engineer,* "Yosemite Lodge—Respectful Companion to Nature." January, 1960.

Sweeping curve of entrance roof offers an outstretched hand to the visitor, beckoning him to enter.

The San Pedro Hacienda well illustrates the principle that building, site, and use must be developed as a unified whole. This was designed to serve the social function of an accommodation for visitors to Los Angeles and local people, allowing them to mingle with one another. This is the result of the efforts of *Richard J. Neutra* and *Robert E. Alexander, architects*, with collaborating design staff: *Dion Neutra, Robert Pierce,* and *Howard C. Miller.*

From the highway it appears as if the motel grew from the hillside. The land-hugging design is particularly well suited to this wind-swept peninsula.

B

A

All guests can have the full sweep of the commanding view through the all-glass building façade.

B

Native ground covers and artful manipulation of grade changes provide excellent marriage of buildings to site.

C

The same dignity, peace, and atmosphere of the lodging facilities pervade the dining area as well.

design is as much a part of the operational balance sheet as heat and light bills.

But, we are digressing from the design process—there is more.

FEEDBACK

Thus far, the steps of analysis, synthesis, and conceptualization have been presented almost as if they were separate and distinct steps. This is not true. Throughout the design of any environment, the design must be kept fluid. All new ideas and information should immediately be brought to bear upon the design.

For instance, it has happened that during the days and weeks spent in the analysis of the project, the city officials passed upon a new plan of highway access—perhaps an overpass right at the proposed motel site. On the other hand, perhaps federal funds came through for renewal of the urban areas including the proposed site. Certainly these must immediately be brought into the design process. This is what we call *feedback*.

Often a by-product of analysis is clarified thinking of the owner. Owners sometimes first believe rather strongly in a certain type and size of motel. They feel that their image is quite clear. As the analysis proceeds, however, many, many questions arise; some answers must be forthcoming. In the process of obtaining the answers, the owner discovers that his first conclusions were wrong and that now he would prefer a different type or size of motel. This is also feedback.

During these first steps, the design team can come onto a new technique or product which allows greater flexibility in the design. Generally, however, these cases are rare if the designers are up-to-date in their technology and thinking. As a result of exchange of ideas among specialists in the design team, new approaches may be extremely desirable. This also is feedback.

To keep the design process from becoming a never-ending one, all feedback must be constructive and not so upsetting as to force a completely new start. This would be evidence of lack of depth in the first steps.

But ideas are not enough. They must be organized in plans if the project is to be built.

PLANS

Although we may have made a detailed study of the site and the business (analysis), tested one against the other (synthesis), and evolved ideas for the development (conceptualization), the project cannot be built without a very important final design step—making plans. Here, we are taking a narrow definition of planning and referring only to the preparation of detailed working drawings, "blueprints," and specifications. These are the vital documents which spell out in complete detail every aspect of the work to be done.

This is much more than just routine office detail, even though this phase uses the greatest amount of the designer's time. It also involves his talents, his creativity, his complete ability and experience. This is the culmination of all the thinking and designing put upon the problem. This is the phase which fixes the theoretical and idealistic approaches of the designer. It is more than hours and hours of drafting time, although an unbelievable amount of time on drafting is needed. It is much more than many hours of conference time among the many specialists in the total design team, which at the time seem almost endless. It is far beyond that which the owner contributes—this is the step in which hundreds of design decisions must be made.

Here the choice is made between steel frame or reinforced concrete construction. Here is decided the amount, color, style of brick, stone, precast concrete, tile—inside and out. Here is decided the size, shape, style of all windows and doors. Here is decided the general nature of the design—strong horizontal, delicate, bold, flowing, rugged, warm, or forceful. And every one of the decisions is made (when properly done) only with full integration of all aspects of the design. The landscape architect's choice of outdoor wall design or sign design must be integrated with the building architect's choices of exterior materials and style. The interior designer's choice of color, texture, and arrangement within the building must be in harmony with the building architecture and present an harmonious foreground when one looks out upon the landscape. These must be accomplished, that is, if the design is to be a success.

Here is the culmination of the designer's art. Here is the full expression of all his talents and abilities. Actually, here the entire project is completed in the mind's eye of the design team. Mentally, every shovel of earth is moved, every board is nailed and every drop of paint is spread—all this before a single bit of construction is started. The project must be not only so well described as to be built, but so carefully worked out that it meets the mechanical, physical, and cultural functions which were described in Chapter 9, "The Meaning of Design."

This, then, is *not* the time for the owner to change his intentions regarding the type of operation. This is *not* the time for him to decide he

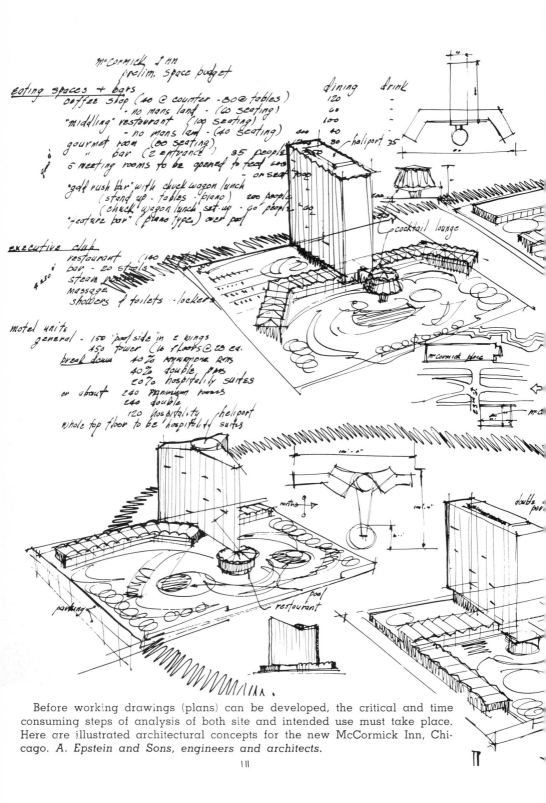

Before working drawings (plans) can be developed, the critical and time consuming steps of analysis of both site and intended use must take place. Here are illustrated architectural concepts for the new McCormick Inn, Chicago. A. Epstein and Sons, engineers and architects.

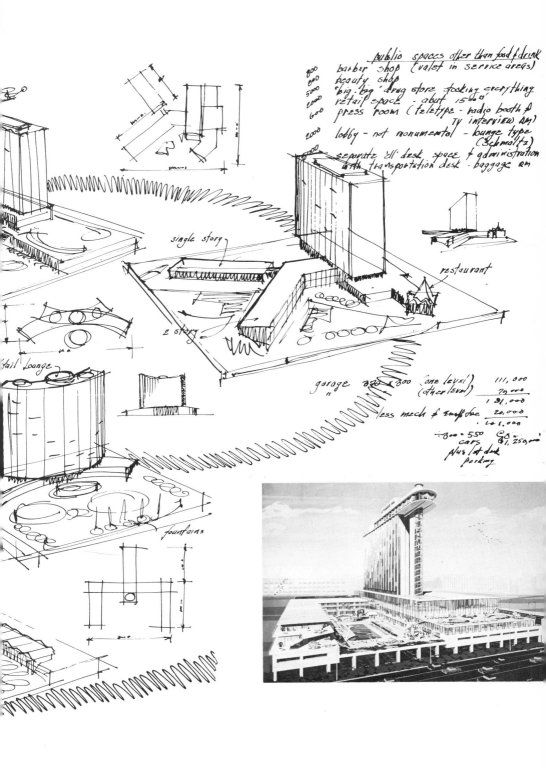

public spaces other than food & drink
800 barber shop (valet in service areas)
800 beauty shop
5000 "big big" drug store stocking everything
1000 retail space - abut 1500 □
600 press room (teletype - radio booth &
                        TV interview Rm)
3000 lobby - not monumental - lounge type
                        (schmaltz)
3000 separate reg'l desk space & administration
     with transportation desk - baggage rm

single story

2 story

restaurant

tail lounge

garage 300 × 300 (one level)   111,000
      "   (other level) 70,000
                                    1,31,000
      less mech & stuff fac 20,000
                                    141,000
      300 × 550 GD
      cars $1,250,000
      plus 1st deck
      parking

fountains

can build a motel only half as large. This is *not* the time for him to be dictatorial regarding details of construction or furnishing. It is too late. These should have been brought into the process earlier. If these topics have not been settled earlier all manner of confusion and difficulty can result. It will mean more office time on the part of the designers—not just to make a few erasures on tracings, but to consider the impact of such changes on all the aspects of planning. The addition of rooms, the changes in layout or relocation of entrances can completely upset all detailing done on grading, footings, plumbing, heating, and electrical systems—to say nothing of the effect on the total appearance and artistic aspect of the whole.

Of course the design team can make such alterations, but one should understand the team's reluctance to do so and the need for additional charges to accomplish these changes at this late date in the process of design. Perhaps by now the first steps of the design process take on great significance and the value of thorough analysis, synthesis, and conceptualization are more clear.

CONSTRUCTION

It may seem strange to add this last step, construction, to the process of design. Are not all the decisions already made? Is not construction merely carrying out the plans of the designers?

Yes, the greatest task has already been accomplished, but even during construction significant design decisions are necessary. As the work progresses, suppose that a strike occurs in the manufacture of a building product or equipment. A decision must be made regarding the choice of delay until the product can be obtained or a substitute product selected. The decision may well affect the design.

Even with the best design approach, last-minute decisions by others can affect a design and both owners and designers are forced into decisions not anticipated. Suppose the motel is abutted by a street under reconstruction and at the last minute the elevation is upped a foot or two. This could have serious impact on the entrance drive location, its grade, and even the elevation of the entire building on the site. Or suppose the backers of the project have financial reverses or go bankrupt just before or immediately after construction is begun. New financial support is sought and the new backers will provide funds only on condition of certain specific changes in design. There is no choice except to make the changes if the project is to proceed.

The only purpose for mentioning these aspects of post-planning design changes is to admit of their happening, and at the same time alert the reader to the need for very thorough execution of each and every step in the entire design process prior to construction.

* * * * * * * *

In summary, the total design process—from motel intentions to open house—is complicated, time-consuming, and at times frustrating. But a process which begins with thorough analysis, utilizes the best of the designer's art, and ends with skillful construction holds promise of great rewards. First among these should be greater guest satisfaction—hence greater financial return to the investor. Of equal value will be the cultural contribution—a designed environment, completely and efficiently fulfilling aesthetic as well as other functions.

Emphasis should be given the element of involvement. At all times, if best results are to be obtained, the owner, prospective manager, builder, and all the design artists must be together on over-all objectives. Their individual responsibilities and activities differ, but if the final motel design is to present a single image to the guest, their efforts must be in the direction of the same goal.

If, through analysis, the owner has a clearer picture of his own motel intentions; if, through analysis, the owner has better knowledge of the site opportunities and limitations; if, through synthesis of motel type and site the owner can reach conclusions regarding his intentions either to quit or proceed; if, through the creativity, imagination, and technical knowledge of the designers a final concept can be developed; and if, by well-executed working drawings and specifications the buildings and grounds can be completed with accuracy—if these phases of the design process have been carried out to their fullest, the results should be far more rewarding than many of the dull, uncomfortable, and unworkable motel designs of today.

Since lobbies and lounges are often the first areas seen by new guests, compelling views of anticipated pleasures represent good merchandising. *Newton Wilds, interior designer;* Lakeway Inn and Marina, Lake Travis, Austin, Texas.

CHAPTER 12

Motel Design Detailia

Standards of motel details have improved so dramatically over the last few years it is difficult to realize that tiled baths and hot and cold running water were rare not so long ago—so rare that they had advertising value and appeared on roadside signs. Therefore, it is not necessary here to present a full course on building construction, except to mention some aspects peculiar to motels. Such omissions here, however, should not encourage the investor, manager, or designer to treat the details lightly. Of all the building types, motels demand the finest of detailing and construction.

LOBBIES

Ever since the *auberge* of ancient times, the lobby of an inn has served a "welcoming" function. Even the motel of today provides an area of welcome (good or poor) near the registration desk. When this function is emphasized, details of size, arrangement and decor naturally fall into place and the arguments for or against seem less serious. It is also well to consider the difference between a lobby and a lounge. The former is essentially an enlarged hallway, providing a pleasant surrounding for the guest to get from the front door to the various functional areas: registration desk, guest room, dining room, manager's office, and other basic areas of the motel. A lounge is a room or area, usually adjacent to the lobby, which serves as a public meeting or semi-public lounging space.

A

A typically compact lobby solution for most small motels: registration desk at right lounge at left, and traffic lanes leading to stairs and entrance. The Gardens Motel, Pine Mountain, Georgia; *Norman Giller, architect.*

A more traditional hotel approach with traffic lanes passing through lounge area to registration desk at right. South Gate Motor Hotel, Arlington, Virginia; *Richard Parli, architect.*

B

In larger establishments, registration will cause little congestion if ample lobby space, as shown here, is provided. Inn at Paris Landing State Park, Buchanan, Tennessee; *Clark and Stoll, architects.*

C

Thoughtful design has made this lounge comfortable, attractive, and semiprivate even though closely tied to traffic areas. Disneyland Hotel, Anaheim, California; *Pereira and Luckman, architects.*

D

A

Another small but inviting lounge, closely related to traffic areas. Huntington Motel, Huntington, Long Island; *Carl Koch, architect,* interior design by *Contract Interiors, Inc.*

B

In a resort-type establishment, it is most desirable to provide a completely separate lounge area for longer-stay guests. The Inn at Paris Landing State Park, Buchanan, Tennessee; *Clark and Stoll, architects.*

A demonstration of lighting the front desk for greatest convenience of the guest and efficiency of management. Golden Gate Motel, Detroit, Michigan.

C

Photo Courtesy of General Electric Corp.

It is a place to wait before entering the dining room or just to relax and read a paper. Many motels catering to largely single-night transients have little or no lounge space. Those catering to conferences and conventions find need for some lounge but far less than the traditional hotel. Probably this is due to the better functionality of the guest room itself.

The accompanying diagram shows the typical functional relationship of the lobby to other areas. No matter the size of the areas involved, the functional relationships will continue to prevail.

Lobbies and lounges need specific interior detailing to provide the kind of welcome the guest responds to. So often one enters a barren, uninviting, bustling area with no apparent connection with the establishment. Through artistic and creative effort, the decor should truly "introduce" the guest to better things beyond—the good night's sleep, the fine meal, the sociability or conviviality of the establishment. A theme should carry his thoughts toward the rooms, dining areas and also toward the grounds. Here is an excellent setting for appropriate murals, but when used they should emphasize local attractions— not an Eiffel Tower or a pyramid for a Chicago motel. The guest should feel that he has arrived and yet feel that more and better things are to come.

A properly designed lobby is easily and quickly mastered by the guest. He should not have to fight his way from window to window or door to door to obtain service. Upon entering, the layout should automatically lead him to the right place.

PARKING

A major aspect of establishing every motel is providing for the guest's car. Solution lies somewhere between the extremes of parking beside the bed or in a lot so distant an attendant must provide the parking service. No matter the solution, it must be solved! And this undoubtedly is the major dilemma of many existing hotels who now find rough competition with the well-lotted motor inn.

As long as land costs permit, owners find solution in ongrade parking. When land costs begin to exceed 15 per cent of the total investment in the entire motel, it is well to consider other possibilities. Partial answer lies in placing the buildings on stilts, allowing the use of most all of the site for parking. The next step is using parking ramp structures, whose cost per guest may be as high as the motel building itself.

Planning for parking is no task for the novice—it demands full understanding of guests' habits and car maneuverability. The wrong barrier, for example, can be completley ineffective and even hazardous to the guest on foot after dark. The layout can confuse the guest, resulting in a car jumble extremely wasteful of space and damaging to both nerves and car bodies.

Considerations of drainage, lighting, position of car relative to the room are extremely vital. In regions of heavy snowfall, snow removal can become awkward and costly if the parking area is poorly planned. Guests resent wading through puddles which so often result from poor engineering of grades. Security and convenience are amplified greatly when the lot is adequately lighted. And how often the blast of noise and exhaust fumes are pointed directly toward the sleeper when the room ventilator is in direct line with the bed and car exhaust.

These continue to be abused in new motel designs and can be avoided with proper thought and skill in the designing stages.

SIGNS—ENTRANCES

A fine steak following an off-flavor appetizer—a dramatic act after sour notes in the prelude—an excellent motel with uninviting, confusing, or battered sign—all these are of the same order. So often high investments in fine facilities are hidden behind a false front.

A common cause of this ailment is lack of understanding that the entrance and sign are an integral part of the business and therefore should be considered so when design work is being done. Advertisers constantly remind us of the power of symbolism—the trademark or emblem becomes a symbol of the product or service. Why not the motel entrance and sign?

The nature of the detailing, the scale, the colors, the arrangement should be designed in complete harmony with the motel building and site. This produces a unity, a singularity of purpose which evokes the singular response necessary if the traveler is to become a guest. More generous sites present greater opportunity for entrance development and should capitalize on this advantage. No matter how large or small, however, the entrance should hold out the welcoming hand and hopefully a pull inward.

Signs and entrances need the skilled touch of those capable of squeezing every possible bit of appeal, enticement, and good taste from the situation.

A pleasant welcome to the weary traveler is here offered by the landscape design of the approach. Heart of Atlanta Motel, Atlanta; *Martini and Associates, landscape architects.*

A   Appropriate unto itself, this entrance demonstrates that the thematic design of the whole is of extreme importance in relating entrance to motel lodging. Disneyland Hotel, Anaheim, California; *Pereira and Luckman, architects.*

B

Another approach to thematic design; the sign has been closely related to the building design. Western Village Motel, Phoenix.

C

A modern caravansary offering an inviting front design and simple announcement on entrance sign. Note repetition of tree-form in architectural forms. Caravan Inn, Phoenix; *Ashton and Wilson, architects.*

The Motel Martinique, Columbus, Georgia, offers this intriguing façade to the traveling public. Note the geometrical design of half-circles on the entrance wall. *Brookbank and Murphy, Architects and Designers; Landscape Architect, Edward L. Daugherty.*

An open to the weather drive-in window for a motel. Southgate Motel, Arlington, Virginia; *Richard Parli, architect.*

The geometrical designs and roof pattern of the exterior of the Martinique Motel are then brought inside as shown in these views of the lounge and dining room. A similar design motif is carried on the menu covers, book matches and letterheads.

A

B

A repetition of the roof design for the pool and patio provides further design harmony and unity—here between the public and private area of the motel.

C

D

A

A modern version of the porte-cochere of olden horse and carriage days. Registration entrance to The Charterhouse Motel, Annapolis, *Victor Gruen, architect.*

The same entrance, revealing its sparkling and warm welcome at night.

B

Here the designer chose to make the most of roadside appeal with a checkerboard wall motif. This might have been too much of a good thing had it not been softened by the sheltered registration entrance. Note design of calling card and match book keyed to that of the motel—symbolism in advertising. Golden Host Motor Lodge, Sarasota, Florida; Schoeppl, Frese Associates, architects.

C

B

4675
NORTH TAMIAMI TRAIL
SARASOTA, FLORIDA
PHONE EL 5-5141

A

While garages have become almost obsolete in most motels, covered porches for car protection against sun, rain, or snow are appreciated by the guests when offered. Desert Caravan Inn, Spokane, Washington; *Victor Wulff, architect.*

B

The strong horizontals created by the continuous balcony enclosures help make the three-story height more acceptable. This smooth adaptation to grade change maximizes the number of rental units without appearing so from the front.

C

For many travelers, the nostalgic flavor of past styles has more appeal than contemporary architectural expression. Downtown Hotel Courts, Mobile, Alabama; *Richard Vander Sys, Architect.*

A

B

Dusk and night impressions of motels are as significant as in daylight. Entrance drives, signs, and buildings cannot carry their messages of invitation and sales appeal at night unless properly lighted. Heart O'Denver Motel, Denver, Colorado; Somerset Inn, Cleveland, Ohio; Marriott Motor Hotel, Dallas, Texas.

C

GUEST ROOMS

Because most guests assume a better-than-average standard of styling, comfort, convenience, and cleanliness, the modern motel room is often judged by its "extras." The pictures on the wall, exposed beam ceiling, and the colors used in the walls, floors, and furnishings now often convert a traveler into a guest. He responds favorably to the glass wall facing toward the patio and generously draped when privacy is desired. He notices the convenience of ample and decorative lighting where he needs it most. He is sometimes "sold" with gadgets, such as pillow-speakers or light controls at bedside. Apparently he now takes for granted that the floor will be carpeted, that the bath will be tiled and that there will be a desk-vanity with generous mirror above. He assumes that all rooms will be furnished with easy chairs, luggage racks and the finest mattresses.

And so, we have run the circuit. To the businessman of a past generation, the large city hotel meant the ultimate in luxury. Its chandeliered and festooned dining rooms and lounges and its thick ornamental carpeted rooms with marble-topped lavatories were out of reach of the rank and file. For them, the one-bath-per-floor hostelry was the limit of the expense account.

Why this flashback into history? Just to remind ourselves of the changes in demand lest we fall into a stereotype of "the best motel room." Just because the market for deluxe rooms has increased in recent years, we shouldn't forget that changes are continuing. Ask any supplier of consumer goods, especially the car manufacturer. This is not to suggest that the old grading of first, second, or third class facilities is in order but to emphasize the need for recognizing various types of demand whenever expressed by the public. Can one facility, with its own fixed location, building design, atmosphere, and management be all things to all people? We doubt it and call the reader's attention to the relative ease of obtaining high occupancies in 10 new motels of 100 rooms each as compared to one with 1,000 rooms. Perhaps this is the trend in attempting to satisfy the stratification of demand as it now appears and continues to grow.

But, back to details. In terms of basic dimensions, the modern motel room does not vary significantly from the finer hotel rooms of 30 or 40 years ago. A modular width of from 12 to 14 feet seems to be optimum, providing for the greatest number of units in a given building length and yet not crowding the room interiors. Recent improvements in fur-

Another view of model motel room, combining TV with writing desk.

A

The studio type room removes all hint of bedroom atmosphere, and is well appointed for conference or entertainment. Deluxe feature is private patio, especially suited to more temperate climes. Disneyland Hotel, Anaheim, California; *Pereira and Luckman, architects.*

B

A suite of rooms is popular with families and some group trade. Careful planning is required to provide private access to bathroom from all sleeping areas. Motel Parkroyal, Melbourne, Australia; *Theodore Berman, architect.*

C

Expression of typical mo- **A**
tel room comforts: carpeted
floors, desk-vanity with ample mirror, desk lighting, tiled
bath. Prairie Traveler Motel,
Bloomington, Illinois; *Lun-
deen and Hilfinger*, architects.

Contemporary simplicity of
line combined with warm
colors and textures is illustrated in this model motel
room for the Howard Johnson
chain. Designed by *Contract
Interiors, Inc.*

Modern motels often offer a two-compartment bath with built-in lavatory, convenient counter space, generous mirror, and lighting of suitable quality, amount, and color. Holiday Inn, Fort Smith, Arkansas.

A

Courtesy of General Electric

B

Impressions of interminable corridor length can be minimized greatly by breaking up the design and intentionally varying the lighting. Motel No. 128, Boston, Massachusetts.

Courtesy of General Electric

Motels in pleasant sur-   *A*
roundings are beginning to
include planning which ori-
ents rooms toward such
views. Here the guest looks
out upon Mountain Creek
Lake. The Gardens Motel,
Pine Mountain, Georgia; *Norman Giller, architect.*

Greatest change in motel
history has been in bath design. Better lighting, ample
mirrors, better ventilation,
and more easily maintained
surfaces are now taken for
granted. Andrew Motor
Lodge, Jasper, Alberta, Canada; *Blakey, Blakey, and
Ascher, architects.*

B

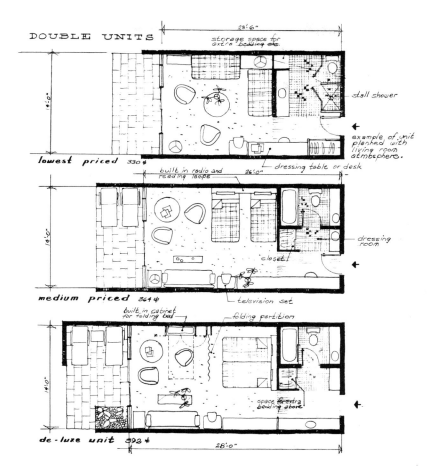

Architect's sketches of room design proposals illustrating a range
of clientele. Greater freedom of building design and structural econ-
omies result from maintaining a width module. *Victor Gruen, architects.*

nishings, such as narrower desks and luggage racks, have done much to
increase the effective width of such rooms.

Basic economics of investment versus returns has forced one major
conclusion: the elimination of the "single" room—one which cannot be
rented to more than one person. With modern construction costs, the
slight additional investment for the added room depth, with almost no
increase in any other costs (windows, doors, baths, etc.) is well worth
it, considering the increased flexibility of renting potential.

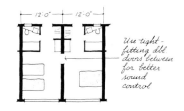

CONNECTING ROOMS

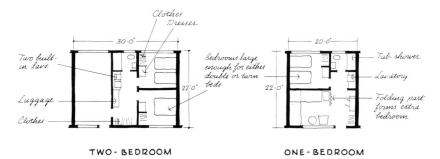

TWO - BEDROOM   ONE - BEDROOM

Typical rooms patterns as observed by the authors. Even a minimum room should be large enough for twin beds or two double beds. The connecting door, one-bedroom, and two-bedroom solutions are in response to the variable nature of today's demands upon guest rooms.

To sum up, the modern motel room has an expression, atmosphere and quality which set it apart from all other room types. The "home away from home" theme may be good for promotion but is a false concept for the motel interior designer. It is a special room, designed, built, furnished for, and used by travelers. Only as it succeeds in fulfilling this function does it succeed at all.

FRONT OFFICE

Although common sense dictates certain logical arrangements in this area, problems in planning do appear frequently enough to give this special mention. Errors in layout confuse guests and create inefficiencies in management.

For best results, the front office should be planned around three major functions: *front desk activities; business office activities; and managerial or private office activities.* These functions remain whether the motel is large or small. Apparent differences are merely in the size and number of rooms devoted to each function.

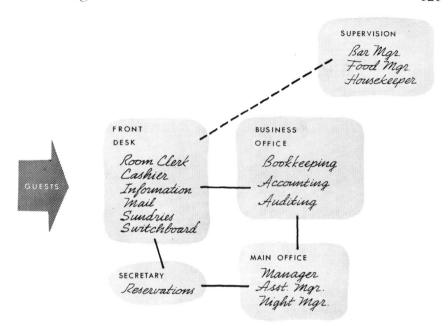

Diagram of functional relationship in the front office. Dotted line indicates a communication linkage but not close physical relationship.

Front Desk Activities

The front desk is the very heart of motel operations. Here the guest is greeted and here all further business between the guest and management takes place. Its arrangement, location, and detailing therefore should express these functions clearly.

It is here that the guests are assigned rooms. Here the many questions of the guests are handled. Here mail is received and delivered. Often here the sales of magazines, newspapers and other sundry items are handled. This is the money exchange point—receiving, paying. For many modern motels, this is also the location of telephone switchboard and teletype.

The completely equipped front office includes the following components:

—Mail rack   —Cashier's station
—Room information rack   —Switchboard
—Key and reservation rack   —Teletype

MAIL RACK

A compartment is needed for each room for the placing of mail and messages. At the bottom provide an alphabetical rack for guest's mail which arrives prior to the expected time of the guest's check-in. Such a supplemental message rack is handy also for leaving notes for your own staff.

We recommend that keys not be placed in the mail rack. Such an arrangement makes the keys visible and reveals the number of vacancies. Also, keys should not be given to anyone without identification. The better plan is to have each room key placed next to each room reservation slot so that the name of each person holding a reservation or already roomed appears adjacent to the key. Then, when someone asks for a key to a certain room, you can verify the occupant of the room before handing over the key.

ROOM INFORMATION RACK

This rack provides quick identification of each room occupant with the names listed alphabetically. A similar rack is needed next to the telephone switchboard for use by the phone operator. Under ideal circumstances the same information rack can be used by the front desk clerk and the phone operator. (In small motels, one person could do both.)

KEY AND RESERVATION RACK

This rack shows all rooms on reservation. A slot for the room key is adjacent to the slip showing the name of the person holding the reservation. Colors are quite helpful in keeping groups intact or to designate special reservations. For example, a group for a meeting or convention could be reserved in red color, V.I.P.'s in green, etc.

Associated with this rack is the advanced reservation book, chart, or cards. Many different systems are available. An easily understood and quickly accessible system is the wall chart. This chart shows all rooms and provides spaces to write the name of the person making an advanced reservation under the appropriate date or dates. Reservations are racked up each morning for the day's expected reservations. In one commonly used system, slips are typed up with the person's name (on the appropriate color) and placed in the correct slot for the room being reserved. This process is sometimes referred to as "blocking."

CASHIER'S STATION

If you use an accounting machine-cash register, this provides a center for this area of the front desk. A locked drawer or cash box is needed if no cash register is used. Any motel over 40 rooms could profitably use an accounting machine-cash register. This machine provides the most complete cash control and greatly simplifies the gathering of financial data. The time and labor saved in the accounting process will probably pay for the machine over its normal useful life. Also, guests like the machine-printed receipt form, which gives a very business-like impression of the motel.

Various business forms are needed such as receipts, vouchers, paid outs, petty cash forms and similar items. A typewriter is also handy for preparing room reservation slips, information and rooming slips, and the headings for the guests, account form (sometimes called a folio).

SWITCHBOARD

The space requirement for your switchboard depends on the number of circuits and the type of telephone service. The new type direct-dial phones require a considerable space for the equipment. Part of this equipment can be placed in a basement but needs particular temperature and humidity control. The type of service where all calls are regulated by the switchboard in the front office may require a very compact switchboard which can be placed right on the front desk. Whatever system is provided space requirements should be known before building. Your telephone company will be pleased to provide full information. The switchboard at which an operator is seated needs to be accessible for service, and this should be considered in your plans also.

If you are installing the new direct dial phone system, a considerable space is needed for the automatic equipment and the meters for reading the toll charges.

TELETYPE

Many motels now have a teletype and this facility will probably become more necessary in the future. A teletype is like a long distance telephone, except that the messages are communicated by writing rather than by spoken words. Some referral associations require teletype service. A directory of teletype users is available, and a motel having teletype can obtain the call number and send a message to any other motel having a teletype. Chain motels customarily have this service, as a considerable part of their business comes from other motels in the chain.

The teletype machine is handier to use and requires less effort if it is raised high enough off the floor so that it can be employed without the operator's being seated. The operator thus can step over to the teletype and write the message without having to get in and out of a chair.

Business Office Activities

In small motels, business office activities are combined with private office and desk, but larger motels require additional space for bookkeeping, auditing and accounting personnel and their activities. The business office should be set apart from the public, but logically should have close physical relationship with the front desk and the manager's office.

The business office is often slighted in new motel planning, especially when the motel grows. Often it is easy to build more units but extremely difficult to expand a central business office.

Managerial Office Activities

In addition to the motel manager and his assistants, in larger motels other members of management require some office space. Usually the housekeeper, food service manager, mechanical engineer, and bar manager prefer a small office near their functional areas. This keeps them in close contact with their responsibilities and usually out of contact with the public.

The manager, his secretary and immediate staff have functions with both the public and other staff. This makes it necessary the manager's office be located not far from the front desk and the business office.

HEATING AND AIR CONDITIONING

In spite of increased engineering technology, this is an aspect of buildings—especially motels—yet to be conquered. Perhaps better systems are available but infrequently used. Maybe they cannot be offered at today's market prices. Whatever the reason, this aspect of comfort has progressed not far since the gas space heater age of early moteldom.

Somehow engineers have yet to reckon fully with the facts of guest comfort, where scales and dials mean little. And admittedly guests are fickle. The winter sportsman coming in from the ski slopes shoves the thermostat upward as the guest next door, in the afterglow of an extended cocktail hour, pushes it down. The guests dressing for dinner want dry air to protect the neatly pressed pleats and trousers, whereas the soaker next door lets the hot water spray from the shower until the entire room is a veritable steam bath. The summer lounging tourist appreciates air in motion for its pleasant cooling effect, but the winter guest stepping from a shower is uncomfortably chilled by it. Reduction of costs sometimes dictates central systems of heating and air conditioning whereas good odor control and quick room temperature response sometimes favor individual air conditioning units. But often the noise of circulating blowers and fans or noisy on-off controls prevent a restful night's sleep.

Yes, we are a contrary lot when it comes to room comfort but just as the gourmet seeks and is satisfied only with fine food, so the motel guest seeks room comfort and the more nearly to his taste that we can provide suitable air—suitable temperature, humidity, odor and cleanliness—the better will be our service to him. And the motel business is a service business.

SOUND CONTROL

Recently, it was reported that a newly-built auditorium was being "tuned." So must motel rooms be "tuned" if they are to allow proper hearing of desirable sounds and yet eliminate those that are undesirable. But there is no magic tuning knob to be turned or slide to be moved. The tuning, or more properly the sound control, is a result of a complex of construction, furnishing, and operation. All sound control problems of a motel are not eliminated simply by adding acoustic tile to the ceiling, even though this may be a necessary part of the entire solution.

Motel sound control begins with the site. Noisy neighboring businesses, railways, airways, expressways can be nuisances. Site arrangement sometimes can help, but little reduction of nuisance will take place unless some solid construction or earth mound is built between the sound source and the motel. Obviously this is difficult to accomplish, but experience with trees or permeable walls has been disappointng. A building parallel with the highway is the noisiest; right angles to the highway, especially when flanked by buildings on both sides, is more suitable. Outside nuisance sounds produced by management (lawn mowing early in morning—shouting to staff) are inexcusable.

Sound control within the building is the task of a specialist in this field because of the many nuisance sound sources and the difficulty of control. Some sounds, such as a reasonable amount of plumbing noise, are tolerated by guests whereas conversation from room to room must be controlled. Within the building, troublesome sounds can be reduced appreciably by careful planning, proper construction, and the right selection of equipment. Obviously, it is extremely difficult to incorporate sound control measures in an existing building without major reconstruction or replacement of equipment.

Basic wall construction, purposely high in sound control (40 to 50 decibels, transmission loss), is the best preventive of troubles between rooms. But any cracks, openings (around connecting doors, heat pipes, wiring) defeat all such efforts at control. Calculations on transmission loss should be made before plans are approved for construction. But walls are not all.

It is desirable to "blot" up sound within the rooms for greater comfort within them and to reduce transmission problems. Extensive use of draperies, the bedspreads, the carpet on the floor and acoustically treated ceilings are effective in this regard. Floor and ceiling control become increasingly important in two- and three-story buildings.

It is easy to make the statement that one should purchase air conditioning, heaters, blowers, pumps, and other mechanical equipment which are quiet in operation, but another thing to accomplish. How can one be assured? By advertising claims? By word of the installer? By experience of existing installations? To a degree, all of these are helpful. Any way of reducing this problem should be pursued. Some manufacturers provide extra mountings for better sound absorption. Separate enclosures or special rooms for equipment sometimes must be provided. Duct work can be designed and lined to reduce the carrying of blower sounds to rooms and conversation from room to room.

Avoid other sound annoyances, such as clothes hangers on back of doors or wall hangers not properly sound isolated from the wall. Adjust telephone bells; install silent door closers; and put maximum volume controls on radios and TV sets.

Put forth every effort possible to keep all problems of sound nuisance at the minimum.

GROUP MEETING ROOMS

When catering to businessmen, there often is call for meeting or conference space. Sometimes beverages or snacks are catered into such areas. Before providing this space, any manager should have ample support for their being included in the plans. For most salesmen, the "sample room" of past hoteldom is not needed—the modern guest room usually does this job.

However, if there is apparent need for meeting space and conferences are being lost to other cities because this is not available, it should be considered. This is costly space to build and generally cannot bring in much if any revenue. Cost of construction and operation must be justified on the basis of increased occupancy and increased food and beverage sales.

Meeting rooms should be planned to include the following important considerations:

—Adequate lighting—controlled for showing films
—Ample ventilation
—Good sound control
—Planned exhibit space
—Ample electrical outlets.
—Spotlights
—P. A. system
—Controlled temperature, heating, cooling
—Comfortable, collapsible chairs and ample ash trays. Folding tables and easels should be stored nearby.

SWIMMING POOLS

While agreement is far from complete on their value, no one can deny that swimming pools are being built at a greater rate than motels themselves. As motelmen debate the issue, the public is being offered greater and greater opportunities for using pools at motels.

Reasons cited by motelmen against installing swimming pools are many and quite sound. Some refuse to turn over valuable land which may be needed for expansion—others simply do not have the land. Some are concerned, and rightly so, about the increased liability. The general public is lawsuit-happy these days and most always win against owners of service businesses. Many feel that the increased capital investment (equal to 1-3 new motel rooms) together with added operating expenses will require a rate increase. Is this good for business? In northern climates where summer tourist business is high the argument for a pool is less convincing because it is less likely to bring business when it is needed most.

But arguments in defense of pools are equally vigorous and the evidence points toward pools being essential in the modern high class motel. First, they *do* bring business, especially families and the younger set. Even the lone salesman appreciates a cool refreshing dip after a hot day of work. But more than this, we are social creatures and like to be with the group even if we never wet a toe. In other words, the pool offers a focal point for gathering, lounging, and getting acquainted. This is a feature motel men have missed since the hand water-pump days of the first tourist camps. It is a landscape feature which can, and most often does, add beauty to the motel grounds. (Exception: some ugly contraptions are sometimes used to cover pools at northern motels in winter.)

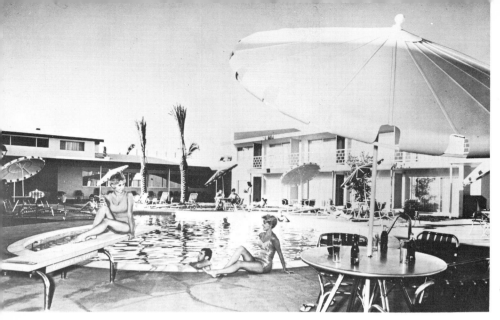

At many motels the entire court area between buildings is paved with a swimming pool as focal point for outdoor recreation. Caravan Inn East, Phoenix, Arizona; *Ashton and Wilson, architects.*

This same patio around pool dramatizes the outdoor setting for events such as the band concert shown here.

For motels, the size and design of the patio is as significant as the pool itself. Hotel Stardust, Yuma, Arizona; *Lloyd T. Williams,* architect.

A

B

Further evidence of the importance of terrace details. Generous lounge space is essential. Due to the difficulty of mixing tiny tots with older swimmers, many motels are turning to the use of wading as well as swimming pools. South Gate Motor Hotel, Arlington, Virginia; *Richard Parli,* architect.

Not all pools must be rectangular nor round, but can be keyed to the degree of informality of the motel. Western Village Motel, Phoenix, Arizona.

A

Water has many decorative as well as practical uses, enhancing motel design. Here a small ornamental pool was incorporated into the landscape design by *landscape architect, Raymond Page*.

B

But no one can miss the point that a swimming pool is in the modern idiom and has sales promotional value. And, finally, a pool adds to the resale value of the establishment.

A motel pool should be:

—beautiful in appearance through its design, setting, access;

—large enough for the maximum number of swimmers, but great size is not necessary. It is more important for the pool to be

—surrounded by ample patio space, lighted, protected from winds, for loungers and watchers;

—enclosed and heated in climates where seasonal patronage demands it;

—built for durability and easiest upkeep; repairs and changes are costly;

—built for safe use (most state health departments have rigid rules governing design, construction and operation of swimming pools).

PART III

Successful

Management

After the fanfare of open house, the glamor of newly polished chrome and tile, and the pride of fresh ink on name cards and letterheads, then what? Is management truly able to settle down to the humdrum routine of renting rooms, cleaning them, and renting them again? Is management ready to face the thousandth guest with the same fresh enthusiasm and attitude of service as guest number one?

Then, depending upon the size of the motel, there is staff to be concerned about. There is staff to be hired, satisfied, and sometimes fired. Has the business established the reputation of a good place to work? Is there good rapport and respect between employer and employees? To what extent is this business dependent upon automation rather than the human factor?

Advertising and promotion are much talked about but generally confused in moteldom. Can a motel afford to advertise, or is it a matter of affording not to? What kind of media are effective and what does an advertising agency do?

And then there are taxes, laws, housekeeping, insurance, just to name a few of the less glamorous but necessary aspects of motel management. And, finally, how does one become proficient in management? These are some of the important topics emphasized in the remaining chapters.

CHAPTER 13

The Human Factor

Unless you as manager have a very small motel. you must hire employees. Your success will depend on how well these employees perform, as they represent *you* to the public. You can't do everything and be everywhere. You thus must depend on good employees to represent you—and do the kind of a job YOU would have done.

In fact, the employees constitute a most important aspect of the business. The following suggestions, if followed, should provide the basis for excellent employee management.

Human relations is an art and those who practice it must cultivate it as an art and constantly keep working to increase their proficiency.

Our greatest opportunity for the improvement of performance and results is through our improvement in human effectiveness.

In order to achieve more effective relations with our employees, we must understand human relations and its application to business. Such an increase in effectiveness is important not only for our own satisfaction and the increase of our own efficiency but is absolutely essential if we are to stay competitive.

BASIC FUNDAMENTALS

If we carefully study the basic fundamentals and apply them to our business, they will help to achieve more profits, happiness and satisfactions. We can equip our supervisors and employees with attitudes, understandings and habits which will result in constructive and coopera-tive workers. We will build our business by our improved abilities to deal with our employees and our guests.

Basic to our better understanding of human relations are some funda-mental aspects or principles relating to human nature:

1. *We depend upon one another.* In this modern complex society we are truly interdependent for our economic life. As long as we are depend-ent upon others, we must do everything we can to make each person's contribution a full one.

2. *Men are social creatures.* We are sensitive to considerations of pride, achievement, desire for esteem and affection. These are all non-economic drives. Men are psychological—not logical creatures.

3. *All men have a sense of justice and conscience.* They are con-stantly making judgements and determining whether decisions regarding employees are equitable.

4. *Management has a moral and social responsibility—a trust to society.* Good wages and stable employment are not the only require-ments for today's employer. He has the additional responsibility of pro-viding satisfying social opportunities for his employees as well as a moral environment conducive to their best interests.

MAN'S BROAD DRIVES AS THEY APPLY TO THE MOTEL BUSINESS

Basic aspects of personality need to be fulfilled in the daily working situation. When all of these are met, workers will be happy, cooperative, and productive.

1. *A sense of dignity and self-esteem.* Every man has rights and feel-ings that others must respect. These rights must be incorporated into any job, regardless of the nature of that job.

2. *A need for the esteem of others.* Each employee must feel that his job is important and that it is important in the eyes of other workers. He craves recognition from others and his job must be so constituted that he can receive this recognition.

3. *A desire to live and to be secure.* The basic needs for food, cloth-ing and housing are of course essential and each employees has the de-sire to be secure now and in the future.

4. *A wish for group association.* He would like to mingle with others having the same common interests.

HUMAN RELATIONS AND MANAGERS

In managing managers, some of the fundamental aspects are as fol-lows:

1. *Management must be by objectives and self-control.* All managers should be placed in a situation where they are striving to reach desirable objectives. Accomplishing these will help build the success of the manager. In order to do this, he must have the proper degree of self-control. Building self-control is the keystone to successful management at any level.

2. *There must be the proper structure for the manager's job.* The organization must be so constituted that the manager has sufficient authority to produce the objectives which are set forth. Unless he has such a structure and is given sufficient responsibility, he is not likely to be successful.

3. *Managers must work together as a team.* If there are several managers in your organization or subordinate managers who work with the head manager, they must all have the right spirit in order to reach their common goals. This spirit is a combination of vision, practices, attitudes and behavior. If it can be established at the outset, it will endure long after the original owners have become inactive.

4. *Managers need a chief executive and a board of directors.* Managers must be able to come to the proper authority for appropriate decisions. Policies of the organization should be established by directors of the highest possible caliber.

5. *Provision must be made for tomorrow's managers.* The future of the business is absolutely dependent upon the quality of future managers. A definite program for the recruitment and development of future managerial personnel should be a part of every business.

Summary

We must increase our understanding of human relations and incorporate its applications into our business.

We must *earn* the initiative, loyalty, enthusiasm, and devotion of our staff. These cannot be purchased.

The most promising single course of productivity in our organization is the human will to work. This can be enhanced by our study and application of these fundamental principles.

TRAINING AND SUPERVISING EMPLOYEES

The Importance of Generosity and Sincerity

The best way to get cooperation from your employees is to be generous in cooperating with them. The more you give, the more you will receive. In order to establish this reciprocal relationship you must first take

time to study your employees. Find out their individual likes and dislikes, their goals and hopes, their backgrounds and possible problems.

Bear in mind that *sincerity is the keynote to success in handling people*. Employees are quick to detect insincere or flippant treatment.

Your study and use of improved human relations and applied psychology will do much to increase your effectiveness in handling your employees. These skills will also enhance your personality and your relationship to other aspects of the business and social world. They will increase your understanding of human attitudes, raise the productive level of your employees and as a result, increase profits.

Behavior and Attitudes

BEHAVIOR.   All behavior results from causes which are either external or internal. Some examples of external causes are responses to supervision, directives, and posted notices. Internal causes may be of a physical nature and stem from hunger, thirst, fatigue, and similar influences.

No two people experience a situation in exactly the same way. To one person, quitting early or coming in late might be perfectly all right, while another person would consider it to be loafing or a very poor attitude concerning the job.

ATTITUDES.   Attitudes are defined as a "readiness to react," or the way we feel inside in regard to any certain situation.

Attitudes are always directed towards something—an object, person, idea, situation or plan. Thus, when you are building attitudes in your employees, they must be built around the important aspects of the job.

Attitudes can be learned either by experience or by coaching or can be taught by a superior or manager. Each employee can learn that if he adopts a certain attitude he is much more likely to achieve the goals he is seeking.

Emotion or moods affect a person's attitude towards work and responsibilities, creating temporary variations in intensity and output.

People depend on each other and we recognize that some people can do some things better than others. Employees often can do certain jobs better than their supervisors or managers. All of the staff have responsibilities regardless of their position in the organization. *The importance of these responsibilities must be enhanced and built up in every way possible.* For example, you could ask a cook about his suggestions for improving the menu or a housekeeper for suggestions on selecting new furnishings or bedspreads.

Hostilities

If there are ever any hostilities among supervisors, managers, or employees, these should be "talked out" as soon as possible. Do not allow any inner resentments or frustrations to remain in the minds of your staff. Put the facts on the table and get the matter settled as quickly as possible.

Pearls of Wisdom in Training Employees

The following seven pearls of wisdom should be helpful to you in improving your human relations:

Perfecting your self-control is 95 per cent of the art of dealing with employees. If you can achieve this, then you will not make decisions when you are angry or make statements which you wish later you had not made. Constantly work to become an exemplary supervisor. You must tread the narrow path and never do anything which would bring discredit upon yourself or your organization.

Explain thoroughly all matters in which your employees may have an interest. Improve your communications and keep your employees informed as to what is going on and why these things are being done. This is a wonderful morale builder and helps to make each employee feel a part of the organization.

Appreciate and praise whenever you can. Tell your employees what a good job they are doing and how much you appreciate their contribution to the organization. Expressing appreciation and praise does not result in requests for raises. People will respond to praise without necessarily thinking of getting more money.

Rewards not punishment. Work some kind of an incentive system, bonus, or profit-sharing arrangement. This helps greatly to increase productivity.

Listen carefully to the ideas and suggestions as well as complaints of your employees. Keep the channels of communications open. Allow employees their say. Do not interrupt—let them give their story.

Strive to criticize tactfully. First praise some aspect of the job which the employee is doing well. Then show him what he is doing wrong and correct the error.

Make your employee's problems your own. You should know about these problems as well as your employee's hopes and aspirations. If there is any way you can help, do so.

PERFECT YOUR SELF CONTROL

PERFECT YOUR SELF CONTROL

P

EXPLAIN THOROUGHLY

P E

APPRECIATE and PRAISE

P E A

REWARDS NOT PUNISHMENTS

P E A R

LISTEN CAREFULLY

P E A R L

STEP 1 PRAISE SOMETHING

STEP 2 CORRECT THE MISTAKE

STRIVE TO CRITICIZE TACTFULLY

P E A R L S

EMPLOYEE'S PROBLEMS YOUR OWN

"Extra Pearl"

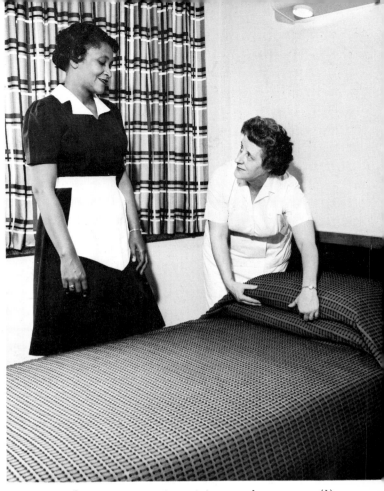

Important steps in training employees are: (1) preparation of the learner; (2) presenting the material; (3) trying out under supervision; and (4) checking back to determine how well the trainee can carry out the task.

All of the foregoing procedures are somewhat contrary to our normal tendencies. To enhance success, we must strive to conduct our relationships with our employees according to these seven basic principles. They all require self-discipline and training on our part.

Steps in Training

1. The first step is *preparing the learner* and this is accomplished by putting the learner at ease when you interview him. Provide a dignified business-like surrounding. State the specific job for which he is hired so that he perfectly understands his responsibilities. Find out what he

knows about the job and the extent of his background and experience. Develop his interests and his desires to learn. Explain the importance of the job and how it fits into the over-all success of the organization.

2.   Step two is *presenting the material* and having ready the things which will be necessary to teach him his job. He should be *told how to do his work and shown how to do it*. Give time for him to ask questions. The material should be presented one main point at a time, clearly, patiently, and in the correct learning order. Special points should be emphasized, so that he is fully aware of the various aspects of the job. Warning: do not present more material than the learner can handle at any one time. It will probably take at least two weeks to fully train the individual even on the simplest job.

3.   The third step is *trying out under supervision*. Now, have the learner undertake the job and verbally point out the main aspects which should be stressed. The supervisor should question him as to why, what, and how so that he is convinced that the learner understands fully the job to be done. This training should continue until you know that he knows the job and knows how to do it right. *Role playing* is a recommended training procedure. The employee practices his job while the manager or supervisor acts the part of the guest. This is especially useful in training front office employees, bellmen, and waitresses—those who contact the public.

4.   The last step is *checking back* to find out how he is performing after his initial training period. Errors should be corrected and reteaching may be necessary. Put him on his own and tell him where to come for help if he needs it. From this point on, coaching can be reduced to normal supervision.

It is often necessary to retrain employees after six months or so because they may develop habits which are not in the best interests of the organization. From time to time courses which emphasize new training techniques and methods should be conducted. (Write to the Educational Institute of the American Hotel and Motel Association, Kellogg Center, Michigan State University, East Lansing, for a list of their excellent home study and group study courses which are applicable to motels). These will help the employee to do a better job. He will appreciate this and develop a higher morale and more satisfactory performance.

Another highly recommended technique is to hold regular staff meetings for all employees. Items of current interest can be discussed and reports made on volume of business, number of guests, upcoming events such as group business, and similar items. This procedure makes employees feel more important and helps them recognize the vital parts which they play in the success of the motel.

CHAPTER 14

Front Office Management

Because of the extreme importance of this portion of the operation it deserves special emphasis. This is the first *business* contact with most guests and therefore the initial time that most guests come in contact with your employees. The entire management will be judged by these first experiences and therefore must be good. Knowledge of the business together with skill are essential for all personnel in the front office. This takes training and practice regardless of whether the owner and his wife serve as front desk people or hired staff members are used.

The primary functions of the front office are: 1) front desk activities; 2) business office activities; and 3) managerial, or private office activities.

FRONT DESK ACTIVITIES

First, the front desk is the contact for *sales*. Here rooms, food service, meeting facilities, and often sundry sales are made. Completing the sale and providing the guest with adequate guidance to rooms is a function of the desk. In addition, it provides *information*. Often this is the first contact the guest makes with the entire community. Here he seeks guidance on places, events, persons, and directions to them. This type of information is equally important to the basic information on the motel—its rooms and other services. This automatically makes the front desk the *hospitality* center. This is where the guest is greeted upon arrival and given a friendly farewell upon departing.

In addition, the front desk is the center for *mail, keys, cashier, telephone switchboard,* and sometimes *teletype.*

BUSINESS OFFICE ACTIVITIES

In the small motel, this function may take place at the front desk, but as the size of motel increases, more private space is needed for it. This becomes the place for *reservations, bookings, and cancellations.* This is the *accounting* and *financial* center. Here are assembled basic financial data on operations. The handling of monies, checks, change bank, and the safeguarding of cash take place here.

MANAGERIAL ACTIVITIES

The management functions have close relationship to the foregoing activities and should be considered in connection with them, even though the offices may not always be grouped together.

Suggestions on arrangement and planning of the front office are presented in Chapter 12. For more information on front office management, references should be consulted.[1]

SELECTING FRONT OFFICE PERSONNEL

The job of hiring and training requires careful preparation. There are three main sources of employees: friends in the motel business who can usually recommend people; trade journals and local newspapers are media for advertisements; and lastly the employment agency. The prospective employee should be given an application to fill out. Depending on the complexity of the operation, a general intelligence test could be given covering reasoning ability, simple mathematics, and English grammar. Persons meeting your recommended levels on these exams whose references reply favorably should be considered for employment. Tests can be obtained through your state university department of psychology.

Desk clerks must be well groomed. This is a basic must since your front office personnel will be in the public eye at all times. Your clerk must also dress well and possess self-confidence in his or her ability to sell the product—*rooms.*

[1]Dukas, Peter, *Hotel Front Office Management and Operation.* Dubuque, Iowa. Wm. C. Brown Co., Publishers, 1960.
Heldenbrand, H.V. *Front Office Psychology.* Evanston, Illinois. The John Willy Company, 1944.

Because smaller motels are less formal, they will require a man or woman who is a jack-of-all-trades. He or she may be called upon to do everything from selling to cleaning rooms.

The larger the motel, the more people you'll have to hire and train. Larger motels usually have two or more people working shifts and a night auditor handling the third watch. The largest motor hotels will subdivide their front office into separate divisions—rooms, accounting, reservations, and switchboard.

Regarding salaries, it is always better to pay a little more for a good person than a little less for a mediocre one.

TRAINING

The motel owner is expected to pay the trainee while he is learning. The employer in most cases uses the demonstration and role-playing methods of training. He will demonstrate the job and explain why it is done this way. Then the trainee tries his hand at the job. Finally, the instructor should *tactfully* correct the trainee regarding any errors and keep careful supervision over him until the trainee can continue to do an excellent job under normal supervision. Use the 4-step plan described in Chapter 9.

Scheduling the front office employees is an important matter. The 7 A.M.–3 P.M. and 3 P.M.–11 P.M. shifts are the two most desirable to the employee and are rotated every two weeks. This familiarizes your clerks with many aspects of the business. Such scheduling also eliminates the feeling of partiality in an individual who works the shift of his or her choice while other clerks are dissatisfied with their hours.

The smaller motel may have to fill only the night shift. In this case, it is best to get a good, reliable, sober man who can be counted on to show up for work regularly. You may also need a swing man in any type of operation to fill in for individuals on their day or days off. This depends on whether your people work a 40- or 48-hour week.

The front office clerk is the motor or driving force which makes the wheels of your business turn. These people will sell, make reservations, confirmations, keep accounting records, and be able to operate all the machines in the front office.

CONDITION OF EMPLOYMENT OF FRONT OFFICE PERSONNEL

1. Employees report to work 15 minutes prior to the start of duty.
2. No drinking on duty.

3. No reporting to duty under the influence of alcoholic beverages.
4. No loitering around the motel after hours.
5. No gossiping while on duty.
6. No entering of guest rooms (except in line of duty).
7. Keep your problems at home.
8. Come to work neatly and conservatively dressed.
9. No gum chewing while on duty.
10. No smoking in front of guest.
11. When addressing guest and fellow employees, BE POLITE!
12. When asked to do something, do it then!
13. No food allowed behind desk (except in case of no relief or night auditor).
14. Reading of literature permitted when all filing and additional work are completed.

HANDLING RESERVATIONS

1. Enter reservation in reservation book upon receipt of the request. Book should have a space for the individual's name, date received, reservation date, type of room, amount of deposit, if any, confirmed or not, reservation guaranteed or held until 6 P.M.

2. After entering, amend data in book for correct day or days of reservation. Enter identical information on a white file card and place card in reservation file by the month. This way you have a double check on all reservations. A chart can be used also.

3. Send a post card or letter reply to the guest immediately, acknowledging his reservation (if time permits).

4. At the beginning of each month, count your rooms reserved for each day of the month. See if you can book supplementary business to fill in available rooms.

5. The first shift each morning will block the rooms for that day. Clerk should check the stay-overs and place the reservations on cards or slips for the rooms which the people will occupy upon their arrival.

6. In the case of overbooking be sure to get the people reservations at a comparable establishment at the price desired, if you have no rooms when they arrive. (Overbooking is considered a risky practice but is sometimes done.)

There are three types of reservations most commonly received by motels: (1) Reservations without advance payment. These are held until 6 P.M. (2) Advance payment reservations are held until arrival. This presents no problem since you already have the money. (3) Guaranteed reservations. This type is done on a contract basis by a company or individual and the rooms are held whether occupied or not.

The guest registration form should contain all the information you require for good management:

1. Name
2. Account number
3. Date
4. Name of street, city, state
5. Room number
6. Rate
7. Number in party
8. Expected length of stay
9. License number of car, city, state, car type, year
10. Clerk's initial
11. Reason for stay (to be entered on guest history card. This card should be immediately available).
    a. Special event
    b. Sports event
    c. Referral
    d. Signs
    e. Tourist attraction
    f. Other forms of advertising being tested
12. Remarks

Be sure the card is completely filled out by the guest when he registers. If he has a wife and children, or others in the party, place all of the names somewhere on the face of the card.

GUEST HISTORY FILE

The guest history card has several uses. It provides:

1. Quick references to credit rating, preferences, previous stays, and guest room patronage.
2. Check of likes and dislikes of guest during previous stays.
3. An accurate mailing address for repeat business.
4. Name and address for promotional campaigns.

Guest histories have been used for years very profitably in resorts and there is no reason why they should not be useful in motel management. Have cards quickly available so that when guest steps up to desk you can immediately check on whether he has been there previously and if so, what room he had. You can say, "Mr. Brown, would you like room 28 again."

For promotional purposes, guests appreciate the little extra effort you have put forth to send a Christmas card or a summer travel brochure. They will very often compliment your efforts by being guests again.

MESSAGES

Once the guest is registered into the motel, it is important to handle all messages. In a motel where the guest resides for a period of time the messages and letters are usually *time stamped* and placed in the guest's mail compartment. If the guest is staying overnight the desk clerk will see that the item is placed in the guest's room or a message is sent to the guest concerning the message which is waiting for him at the front office. Message-waiting telephones are great step-savers.

CASHING CHECKS

As a rule, cashing checks is a risky business. The best procedure is to phone the bank to verify the deposit prior to cashing the check. If this is not feasible, some reliable identification is advisable. A credit card is good, but drivers' licenses are not very dependable. If a check is accepted and subsequently returned "not sufficient funds" you can sometimes collect it if you resubmit the check at the first of the month. If this fails, send the check to the home address of the person giving the check and ask that payment be made promptly. This may produce results. If this fails, charge it off as a business expense under bad debts.

CREDIT CARDS

In most cases the smaller motel will receive cash payment for the room in advance upon checking in. The larger motels may honor several credit cards. The most widely honored cards are those issued by American Express, Diner's Club, and Hilton's Carte Blanche. Some motels have their own credit cards which they issue to regular repeat guests.

FRONT OFFICE FORMS

Listed following are standard forms needed by motels. Printing and supply houses will send you catalogues which illustrate the forms available. Generally, the following are considered essential:

1. Guest registration cards.
2. Reservation request cards (self-addressed on the reverse side).
3. Reservation acknowledgment or confirmation cards or forms.

4. Room reservation forms or cards (for advance reservations).
5. Rack cards or slips for advance reservations.
6. Rack cards for room condition (on change or out of order).
7. Guest account cards or folios (sometimes printed on reverse side of registration card).
8. Guest ledgers or folios (individual guest's accounts which are payable upon checking out of the motel). May be hand transcript types or used in accounting machine.
9. Guest receipt forms.
10. Guest history cards (for recording each individual guest's patronage over a period of time and any remarks concerning him).
11. Reservation charts, cards, or book (showing all rooms per day, month, or quarter).
12. Safety deposit envelopes (for receiving guest's valuables to place in safe).
13. Telephone message.
14. Message card for guest's doorknob.
15. Long distance telephone calls charge form.
16. Local telephone charge form.
17. Morning call sheet.
18. Letterhead stationery and envelopes.
19. Color postal cards.
20. Mail forwarding cards.
21. Rooming slips (given to guests and includes room number, guest's name correctly spelled, and rate for room).
22. Purchase order forms (standard form for ordering supplies and equipment).
23. Daily rooms report (a daily financial report).
24. Housekeeper's report (on rooms made up).
25. Maid's daily report.
26. Various cash sheets and accounting records. (See the manual *Uniform Classification of Accounts for Motels and Motor Hotels* for titles and standardized financial statements.)

The following concerns supply office forms:

American Hotel Register Co., 230-232 W. Ontario St., Chicago 10, Illinois.

American Printing and Stationery Co., P.O. Box 536, Wellston, Missouri.

Associate Service, 255 Robinson Road, Pasadena 6, California.

Blackbourn Systems, Inc., 230 South Cedar Lake Rd., Minneapolis, Minnesota.

Butler Enterprises, Inc., Drawer 2958, Winston Salem, North Carolina.

Gresham's Manufacturing Stationers, Temple, Texas.

Hotel and Motel Supply Co., 34 North Brentwood Blvd., Clayton, Missouri.

John Willy, Inc., 1948 Ridge Avenue, Evanston, Illinois.

Motel Contract Supply Corp., 6635 Delmar Blvd., St. Louis 5, Missouri.

Motel Printing and Stationery Co., 126 West 21st., Ann Arbor, Michigan.

Specialty Merchandisers, 512 South Main St., Ann Arbor, Michigan.

Whitney Duplicating Check Co., 406 West 31st, New York 1, New York.

SELLING THE GUEST ROOM

All of the capital, planning, construction, furnishings, and advertising of your motel are for naught if you and your front office staff are not expert at selling rooms. Room revenues are the fundamental measure of success. Many a room remains vacant because the personnel of the motel were not adept at making the customer want to buy.

The room clerk may be the official greeter of your operation. A warm *smile* and the familiar greeting of "good afternoon" or "good evening," and "may I show you a room," will always be a good starter for your sale. Creating an impression of cordiality and hospitality is the first and very important step.

The second step is to deal with the prospective guest in a spirit of friendly competence. The clerk must be able to make the guest feel he knows what he is talking about. He must feel that the *best possible room* is being selected for his particular party. When the room has been selected at the desk, offer to show the room. If others in his party remain in the car, invite them to inspect the room also. Upon arrival at the room, open the door and courteously invite the prospect to enter, and follow him in. Comment on the comfortable bed, clean bath and if it is hot weather, the fact that you have air conditioning or fans. In cold weather point out the central heating system, with its individual temperature control.

Rates are a troublesome aspect of selling. Standard rates for each room should be posted in the room for all to see. However, some people will demand to know the rates the minute they step up to the desk. Usually, these demands can be parried by stating that you have different sized rooms with various combinations of appointments and thus have varying rates. Offer to show the room and if you can get the prospect into the room, you can usually sell it. Sometimes this procedure doesn't work and the prospect demands to know the rates, then and there. In this case, you first find out how many are in his party and then quote several rates, i.e., with double bed, twins, suite, and any other possibility which may be available. Always offer to show the room in any event. A bellman or porter may have to show rooms and if this is the case they should be thoroughly trained in selling rooms.

There are times when showing a room is impractical. An alternative is a display of color pictures of the rooms at the desk. Another method is to hand the key to the prospect and let him look at the room on his own. This seems to be quite effective.

In selling rooms, never come down on your rates for any given room. If the prospect objects to the rate and you think he would take a less expensive room, show him another room and quote a lower rate if you wish. Bargaining with guests is a poor policy and tends to encourage "shoppers." This has a debilitating effect on the motel industry and should be avoided.

An excellent little book is available entitled *Front Office Psychology* by M. V. Heldenbrand. It contains many practical suggestions in regard to selling rooms and dealing with guests. The publisher is John Willy, Inc., 1948 Ridge Avenue, Evanston, Illinois.

Always remember to say "thank you" regardless of whether or not you make a sale. Courtesy is the byword of the motel industry and there is never an excuse for discourteous manners. "Thank you" are two words in the English language which motel keepers can never overwork!

GROUP SALES AND PARTY BUSINESS

Individual sales efforts in the community will be most rewarding if well planned. Groups and organizations need the services and facilities which many motels make available.

You should provide some incentive for your clerks to get out and do sales work after hours. Good public relations is always beneficial. You'll find that the clerks who will move up to managers and owners will be those who will devote some of their free time to selling your organization.

AUTHORITY

One of the most important things which every manager should impress on his desk clerks concerns the clerk's authority in cases of absence of the manager.

CHAPTER 15

Better Records

Every motel manager knows that he must keep accurate records of business transactions for tax purposes. In addition, these accounts can provide valuable guides to increased profits.

From the managerial point of view, a good accounting system should:

1. Provide a complete and permanent record of business transactions.
2. Enable the operator to safeguard his assets.
3. Enable him to control every phase of his operations in the interest of profitability.

The first of these requirements is basic. Without the recording of transactions there would be no means of carrying out the major functions of the classification of accounts. The actual method of recording, however, is secondary, for it can be of little value in itself. Only the results of recorded transactions are of value in an analytical sense.

The primary purpose of record keeping is the one stressed in legal requirements. Law-making bodies demand that there be written evidence of the history of a business so that it can be analyzed for tax purposes and other reasons. It has been pointed out by some regulatory bodies that many businessmen are unable to make the best use of these records because they are not kept sufficiently up-to-date to get the needed infor-

---

[1]From *Uniform Classification of Accounts for Motels, Motor Hotels, or Highway Lodges* (Temple, Texas: Tourist Court Journal, 1960).

mation at the proper time. As a result, the other two main purposes of accounting records are defeated.

Second function of a well designed accounting system, i.e., the safeguarding of assets, is exercised through various methods of checks and duplications, and is needed to overcome human error—both intentional and accidental. Many smaller motel operators who own their businesses and operate them with only members of their immediate families may scoff at the mention of a need for a system of check and recheck. They overlook the fact that such a system also will help them detect errors that may be made unintentionally. In addition, this system facilitates the detection of fraudulent activities of hired employees, if such occur.

It is this phase of accounting, the safeguarding of assets, that is lacking in many motel operations. Operators fail to place any significance on depreciation or maintenance policies and find that when the time arrives for replacement of worn-out furniture, linens and fixtures, they are unable to finance properly the necessary replacement items. A very common error in thinking on the part of some businessmen is that cash in the bank and net profits are one and the same.

The third function is that of planning and controlling operations. The motel industry here shares in a problem common to other service-type operations in that its merchandise has a total daily perishability. At the end of a day's operation, any room not rented is merchandise that has perished. The revenue from its rental has been lost forever. If the rate of occupancy which is required for profitable operations drops, the residual amount going to the operator is soon wiped out. If the revenue drops significantly, the uninformed operator can soon lose his investment as fixed charges continue to face him. At the same time the profitability of related income-producing activities, such as the operation of a restaurant or gift shop, must be definitely proven by accurate operating data which can be provided only through good records.

For example, a motel operator must consider the problem of whether to provide kitchen facilities for his guests. His decision should be based on the amount of added revenue a kitchen unit produces over that of a hotel-type room, taking into consideration the increased costs incident to its operation, e.g., china breakage, depreciation and additional maintenance. Another managerial problem which can be solved properly only by careful anlysis of past experiences, as shown by records, concerns what percentage of each room type—double, twin, suite—should be provided.

The specific problems each individual operator must meet will vary, depending in part on his location, type of clientele, seasonal variations and other factors. Each proprietor will be able to chart his own individual business course better, however, if he makes maximum use of his own records as guideposts.

USES OF ACCOUNTS AND
FINANCIAL STATEMENTS

Begin by keeping accounts which are true, significant and applicable. Know why you keep such accounts. Know their value to the well-being of your business. Use this information to improve management efficiency and profits.

Organize your accounts in accordance with the Uniform Classification of Accounts for Motels and Motor Hotels as described in the manual. The accounts have been very carefully formulated to meet all of the qualifications for good managerial application. When there is a food service or other major income-producing department, similar appropriate accounts should be kept.

Use these accounts to provide essential basic data needed in motel management. Study both the daily and monthly reports which will provide you with two types of vital information: (1) Actual dollar results of operating the motel, and (2) the results of any changes you may have made in managerial policies.

In regard to the second point, the only way in which the effects of any new methods or services can be measured is through adequate figures. You may decide to try offering breakfast or some similar new service. But until you have good figures to reflect these changes, you are in the dark as to their effectiveness.

Illustrated following is an example of a 40-unit motel which opened a new restaurant the first of August:

Daily or Monthly Managerial Information

	July	August
Number of rooms	40	40
Number of days in month	31	31
Number of rooms available to guests (40x31)	1,240	1,240
Number of rooms occupied (from sales acc'ts)	915	994
Percentage of occupancy (915 ÷ 1,240)	73.7%	80.1%
Room sales	$6,725.25	$7,455.00
Average rate per room ($6,725 ÷ 915)	$7.35	$7.50
Number of guests registered	1,415	1,522
Average rate per guest ($6,725 ÷ 1,415)	$4.75	$4.89

If this pattern continues, the new restaurant will have a very good effect on room sales and occupancy in the motel. The increase in business also might be due to a more effective sign program, more tourists, or other significant reasons.

Running or cumulative sales — totals for today, month to date and year to date — provide vital management information. For example, the total room sales for the first 10 days in June (month to date) of this year are compared to the month to date sales for the same period of last year. Year to date (cumulative sales for the year up to June 10) are also compared with the last year, year to date. Trends can be determined quickly by this method.

Item	Today	To Date	Year Ago To Date	Month To Date	Mo. to Date Year Ago
Room sales	$220.50	$30,450.00	$28,991.50	$2,205.00	$1,874.50

A quick review of these figures reveals that the trends are quite favorable, as all of the comparisons of room sales indicate an increase over previous periods.

MONTHLY REVENUE AND EXPENSE STATEMENT

In addition to the daily and monthly managerial data, review your very important monthly record of operating expenses and income.

Preparing the monthly Revenue and Expense Statement involves first a summary of room sales for the month. Then list the controllable operating expenses as shown in Chapter 5 under Rate Computation by Costs—Returns Method.

A proportional monthly charge for fixed expenses is deemed essential. These are charges such as depreciation, insurance, taxes, and interest. The final step is a subtraction to determine the amount of profit or loss for the month.

Now, look carefully at every figure on the monthly statement to ferret out any hidden meanings or implications. Why was that amount low? Why was it high? Should it have been lower or higher? What could be done to improve the situation? Try to find answers to these and similar questions.

Important items which should be studied, checked and compared are: (1) Salaries and wages for employees and the efficiency of such employees; (2) Whether expenses are properly classified for uniform comparisons with the industry trends and ratios; (3) Whether rentals paid for use of assets is reasonable and commensurate; (4) Is depreciation realistic and in line with current practice in the industry? (5) Have all risks been covered with insurance of sufficient amount? and (6) Is the level or amount of profit sufficient to provide a fair rate of return on investment?

Next, compare each item on the statement with comparable previous periods. Thoughtfully, check each major item to determine trends. Corrective action can then be initiated, for now the basis for action is a solid foundation of usable financial facts.

A further use of both good individual accounts and of representative trade data is found when the motel operator seeks credit. Bankers and other lending institutions require all the information obtainable in deciding whether to grant credit, and the man who is best informed about his own operations and current trends in the trade is most likely to get the loan, other things being equal.

ANNUAL STATEMENT OF REVENUE AND EXPENSE

This statement should be studied carefully in a manner similar to the daily and monthly reports. This gives you a longer, over-all view of your operating results.

Precise and meaningful interpretations can be made by using a device called a ratio. A ratio is simply a statement of the relationship between two amounts. It is often expressed as a percentage. For example, if room sales were $80,000 and salaries and wages expenses were $20,000, the wage ratio would be 25 per cent.

Now, compute the ratios of each of your expense items in relation to room sales. Ordinarily, sales are considered to be 100 per cent so the ratios of all of the expenses plus the profits will equal 100 per cent.

Next, compare your ratios to several kinds of bases or standards. These standards can be: (1) your own judgment based upon experience and evaluation; (2) past performance found by comparing this period with the same period last year and other comparable periods, and (3) typical performances of other similar businesses as reported in research reports of motel operating statements or averages.

Universal adoption of the Uniform Classification of Accounts for Motels and Motor Hotels will bring about reliable data which can be used with confidence. You know that every manager who is reporting is classifying his financial transactions in accordance with this manual. This adds immeasurably to its value and usefulness because you can see how you are actually succeeding in comparison with similar motels.

BALANCE SHEET

This valuable statement also provides significant managerial data. The successful manager uses the balance sheet to make comparisons of the amounts and the relationships of assets, liabilities and proprietorship (the excess of assets over liabilities). Each part of these three major divisions of the balance sheet is studied and compared to previous balance sheets.

Of particular consequence is the amount of the motel owner's equity of proprietorship. This should show an increase as the business grows and prospers.

REVENUE AND EXPENSE STATEMENT

This outlines in detail the classifications of revenue and expense items commonly dealt with in motel operations. The Revenue and Expense Statement and the explanation of revenue and expense items are presented first because they offer the most important source of sound managerial data for the motel operator.

The Revenue and Expense Statement as found in the Manual is recommended as a standard, uniform statement for the motel industry. It is flexible and can be adapted easily for a motel operation regardless of size. The amount of additional detail of revenue and expense subgroups used or supplemented will depend on the individual operator's obtaining the special or specific information he desires. The Revenue and Expense Statement as presented, however, is sufficiently complete to answer the questions that normally arise in the conduct of a motel operation.

The major elements of revenue and expense are summarized under their logical headings for the preparation of the basic statement but these can be expanded indefinitely to suit special needs. For example, the heading "Employee Wages" may be subheaded for maids, maintenance men, assistant managers, office help, switchboard, etc.

An attempt has been made in the preparation of this manual to list as completely as possible the expense items that can be found under each of the various headings. However, there will always be some types of revenue or expense that have not been specifically mentioned. In these cases, the item should be included in the revenue or expense grouping which contains transactions most similar in nature.

EXPLANATION OF FINANCIAL STATEMENTS

Periodically, you will want to review the results of your business operation and your position at the end of the period. This is the purpose of the two basic accounting statements—the Balance Sheet and the Revenue and Expense Statement.

These two statements are prepared annually for tax purposes, but they should be prepared and reviewed more frequently than one time a year in order to obtain a current and useful picture of your business developments.

The difference between these two basic statements can be explained in photographic terms, that is, the Revenue and Expense Statement is a "moving picture" which gives you the results of your operation over a given period of time. It indicates the revenue for the period and the costs and expenses incurred in the receiving of this revenue. The Balance Sheet, on the other hand, is a "still picture" of your business. It shows your financial condition or position at a specific time and date.

Check List For Analyzing Your
Revenue And Expense Statement

1. *Net Profit*   Yes   No
    a. Is the net profit large enough for size and type   ——   ——
       of business? (The more profitable motels run
       7 to 15 per cent net on investment.)
    b. Is a full charge being made for depreciation?   ——   ——
       (This is usually the largest single item of
       expense.)
    c. Is a comfortable salary allowed for owner-   ——   ——
       manager?
       (In a *Tourist Court Journal* survey, the average
       salary for a man and wife team was $5,600.)
    d. Do you have a sufficient insurance coverage?   ——   ——
       (A basic protection package plan might save
       you money.)
    e. Do you pay too low wages?   ——   ——
       (Minimum wage laws are being emphasized
       in some states.)
    f. What is your long-term trend?   ——   ——
                                    up   down

(Many motels have seen a drop in profits—as a percentage of gross income—in the last three years.)

2. *The Basis for Net Profit*
   a. Are room sales per room per year sufficient? ———— ————
   b. Have you carefully studied each major expense item? ———— ————
   c. Have you compared expense items with other similar motels? ———— ————
   d. Is depreciation expense realistic? ———— ————
      1. Do you have all depreciable property listed?
      2. Do you state actual useful life or rate?
      3. Are you using the most advantageous depreciation method?

3. *Are Any Parts of Your Business Losing Money?*
   a. If you have a restaurant, is it profitable? ———— ————
   b. Are you doing your own laundry? ———— ————
   c. Would linen rental service or laundry service be economical? ———— ————

4. *Are There Sidelines Which Could Add to Profits?*
   a. Gift or souvenir shop, cigar counter, vending machines, or snack shop? ———— ————
   b. Could you do some group or convention business? ———— ————

CHAPTER 16

Taxes and Laws

As long as we continue to demand more services from government, we must pay more taxes. In fact, the amount of taxes paid plays a major role in business management. This is especially so in the case of the federal income tax. Every advantage should be taken of legal tax exemptions and deductions in order to avoid unnecessary taxes. The advice of a competent tax attorney or accountant should be sought early in the life of the business. With adequate records and expert analysis and study, the manager should be able to minimize his tax obligation.

THE FEDERAL INCOME TAX

This tax was first proposed in 1815 and actually collected during the Civil War. However, it was subsequently declared invalid in 1894. The Sixteenth Amendment to the Constitution was passed by Congress on July 12, 1909, and ratified by the required number of the states in 1913. Since this date, over 40 revenue acts and laws have been passed, most of them raising the rates.

Essentially, the federal income tax is a tax on net income, arrived at by subtracting the "ordinary and necessary business expenses" from the gross revenues or sales. The rate of tax is determined by the gross income, deductions for adjusted gross income, other itemized deductions, standard deduction, deductions for personal exemptions, and taxable income.

Depreciation Expense

Whether you hire an accountant or do your own books (or both), you will be confronted with the problem of accounting for depreciation of property. Because depreciation expense is the largest single item or cost in operating a motel, the significance of these accounts in relation to your profits is indeed important. It pays to become thoroughly familiar with the various depreciation methods and the considerations involved in selecting a method or methods.

In addition to the *straight-line method* which has been in most common use, the Internal Revenue Code of 1954 provides two accelerated methods of accounting for depreciation. These methods allow a faster write-off in the early years for capital goods assets having a useful life of at least three years and purchased after December 31, 1953. In the case of buildings, the structure must have been built or completed after December 31, 1953. In the case of an old building purchased after December 31, 1953, any additions and alterations can be depreciated under the liberalized methods, but the cost of the building cannot. More liberalized depreciation provisions were enacted in 1962.

Here are the three principal methods of computing depreciation expense:

The "straight-line" method. This has been the most common method used and it is still authorized (1962). Under this method the cost or other basis of the property, less its estimated salvage value, is deducted in equal annual installments during its estimated useful life.

The "declining-balance" method. This is a new liberalized method which permits a faster write-off in the early years of the property. Under this method the greatest depreciation is taken in the first year of use, with continually decreasing amounts of depreciation in later years. A uniform rate is applied each year to the unamortized basis of the property. The salvage value is not deducted from the cost or basis of the property prior to applying the rate.

The "sum of the years-digits" method. This third method is similar to the "declining balance" method. It is computed by applying a changing fraction to the cost or basis of the property, less its estimated salvage value.

In the fraction used for any one year, the numerator (top of fraction) is the number of remaining years of the estimated useful life of the property. The denominator (bottom of fraction) is the sum of the numbers representing the years of life of the property.

Other methods. Any other consistent method may be used to figure the annual depreciation allowance for property which is eligible for liberalized methods. However, the method used must be such that the total allowances for depreciation at the end of each year do not exceed, during the first two-thirds of the useful life of the property, the total allowances which would have resulted if the declining balance method were used.

SELECTING A DEPRECIATION METHOD

There are a number of important considerations involved in making a decision. It may be to your advantage to use two different methods. This depends on the class of property and your particular circumstances. You can use different methods appropriate to different classes of assets, but you must be consistent with regard to each class.

For example, if you are using the straight-line method in depreciating furnishings, then you must use this method for all furnishings.

The two liberalized methods allow a greater depreciation expense in the early years of life of the property. More expense means less profit. Less profit means payment of less income tax. The resulting reduction in tax will allow the use of these savings for other purposes.

Funds can be used in several ways: (1) for paying off debts, (2) for setting aside in a sinking fund in the form of a separate bank account to be used for eventual replacement of property, and (3) for current expansion or improvements.

Depreciation is a bookkeeping procedure. *Recognition of depreciation expense in the records does not, however, result in providing funds. These funds must be set aside by good management for the uses already outlined.*

With these relationships in mind, the following typical situations are presented in order to determine the depreciation method that would be the most advantageous in each case.

Situation No. 1. The owner of a new motel has just begun operation after an eight-month period of new construction. He has heavy commitments, including payments on his mortgage and cleaning up some personal notes. He thus needs as much ready cash as he can get his hands on.

In this situation, it would be to his advantage to use an accelerated method (probably the declining balance method). This gives him the highest depreciation expense in the first critical years. Later, after he has met some of the most pressing obligations, he can switch to the straight-line method or continue with the declining balance method on the furnishings. In the table, "Comparison of Depreciation Methods," under the declining balance method, it will be noted that the furnishings account at the end of five years has been more than two-thirds amortized.

If he could sell the used furnishings for more than the remaining book value (unamortized cost), the gain would be taxed at 50 per cent (a long term capital gain). If they were sold at less than the book value, the loss would be 100 per cent deductible.

Situation No. 2. This motel operator is expecting a low net profit which may be due to a number of reasons. He may even be expecting a loss. Under these circumstances, it would be to his advantage to use the straight-line method as it provides the lowest amount of depreciation. His expenses, before depreciation, are already high in relation to his income.

The anticipated low net income will require a correspondingly low payment of income tax (or in the case of a loss, no tax at all). By using the straight-line method, a larger amount of unamortized capital goods investment will remain on the books.

Property remaining on the books can probably be amortized more rapidly in the future under one of the accelerated methods. This would be especially advantageous if his income became larger.

He is optimistic and believes that income tax rates may be lower in the more distant future. In this case there would be an additional advantage in the future use of one of the accelerated methods. During the life of the property, the depreciation expense steadily decreases.

A tax advantage would result with a higher net income in these later years. (Permission of the collector is necessary to change methods of computing depreciation, except a change from the declining balance method to the straight-line method.)

Situation No. 3. A motel owner may feel that he can save money on his furnishings and equipment by having a very high standard of maintenance. Refinishing service may be economical or he can do it himself. In this case, there would be no particular advantage in using the liberalized methods.

He would probably keep his furnishings for the full extent of their useful life. Any increase in depreciation expense made in the early years would be offset in the later years, as previously explained.

Situation No. 4.　This fortunate motel owner has his property all paid for. He enjoys a substantial income. His motel is gaining in popularity and it would appear that his income is due to rise over the years. With income tax rates remaining at high levels, he is pessimistic enough to believe that these rates are not going to be materially reduced in the future.

Under these circumstances, it would be to his advantage to use the straight-line method for most of his classes of assets. The reason is that, although the liberalized methods allow a faster write-off in the early years, a consequently lower allowance is necessary later.

If the operator is expecting large future income, he thus would be wise to have this property on the books in order to maintain his depreciation expenses in the future years, with income taxes remaining high.

Another consideration is the possibility of sale of the property. If he anticipates selling, it probably would be to his advantage to use the straight-line method on most classes of property. If he sold at a figure considerably above the book value of the assets, using the straight-line method would tend to reduce the amount of the gain. Thus, the tax would be lower.

COMPARISON OF DEPRECIATION METHODS

Example: New room furnishings. Cost $4,000,
estimated salvage value $500. Estimated useful life 10 years.

	1. Straight line (figured on $3,500)		2. Declining Balance (figured on $4,000)			3. Sum-of-the-Digits (figured on $3,500)		
Year	Annual Deduction 1/10th.	Cumulative Amount Amortized	Balance (Unre-covered) cost)	Annual Deduction 1/5th (twice the straight-line rate)	Cumulative Amount Amortized	Rate (fraction of cost)	Annual Deduction	Cumulative Amount Amortized
1	$350,00	$ 350.00	$4,000.00	$800.00	$ 800.00	10/55°	$636.36	$ 636.36
2	350.00	700.00	3,200.00	640.00	1,440.00	9/55	572.73	1,209.09
3	350.00	1,050.00	2,560.00	512.00	1,952.00	8/55	509.09	1,718.18
4	350.00	1,400.00	2,048.00	409.60	2,361.60	7/55	445.46	2,163.64
5	350.00	1,750.00	1,638.40	327.68	2,689.28	6/55	381.82	2,545.46
6	350.00	2,100.00	1,310.72	262.14	2,951.42	5/55	318.18	2,863.64
7	350.00	2,450.00	1,048.58	209.72	3,161.14	4/55	254.54	3,118.18
8	350.00	2,800.00	838.86	167.77	3,328.91	3/55	190.91	3,309.09
9	350.00	3,150.00	671.09	134.22	3,463.13	2/55	127.28	3,436.37
10	350.00	3,500.00	536.87	107.37	3,570.50	1/55	63.63	3,500.00
			$ 429.50 remains as undepreciated balance. If property is still in use, continue depreciation. The depreciation method can be switched to the "straight-line" method at any time and thus have the asset fully depreciated at the end of its useful life.			°55—sum of the numbers from 1 to 10.		

COMPUTATION

First, you must have the *exact* cost or basis as the beginning point. This should include delivery charges and cost of installation. In the case of buildings, the investment can be allocated among structure, wiring, heating, plumbing, and air conditioning. This is sometimes done in new buildings were exact figures are available from the subcontractors. Reason for the breakdown is that these parts of the building depreciate faster than may be the case of the building itself. The most common method, however, is to place the entire building in one lump sum and depreciate it over an average useful life.

Average Useful Life

The length of useful life of business property is affected by two forces: (1) physical wear and tear and (2) obsolescence due to techno-

Property	Average Useful Life (Yrs.)[1]
Air conditioners (small)	10
Blankets and spreads	6
Carpets and rugs	6
Cleaning equipment	10
Dining room furniture	8
Guest room furnishings	8
Heating systems	20
Kitchen equipment	10
Laundry equipment (commercial type)	15
Lighting fixtures	15
Lighting fixtures (portable)	5
Lobby furniture	8
Plumbing fixtures	25
Power lawn mowers	3
Shades	5
Signs (neon and electric)	8
Springs, mattresses, pillows	9
Venetian blinds	8
Wells and well pumps	25
Motel building (average construction)	25

[1]All estimates are from Bulletin "F," Bureau of Internal Revenue, except guest room and dining room furnishings, signs, and motel buildings. These are estimates of the American Motor Hotel Association. New, more liberalized rates were authorized in 1962.

logical improvements, economic changes, location advantages and other causes which shorten the life.

Past experience provides the best guide. Informed opinions as to the quality and present condition of the property together with current trends and developments within the motel industry should also be considered.

The Internal Revenue Service does not apply depreciation rates arbitrarily; however, they check to see if the rate you use is commonly accepted by the industry as normal and reasonable. Agreements on useful life, method, and rate of depreciation can be made with your district director of internal revenue on Form 2271.

Group accounts can be used for assets which are similar and which have approximately the same average useful life (such as guest room furnishings).

If the estimated life is subsequently found to be incorrect, a change should be made in the rate. The unrecovered cost is then spread over the revised estimated remaining life. However, there must be a clear and convincing basis for redetermination.

The life may differ due to heaviness of use. For example, an air conditioner used in Michigan might be used as little as 30 days in a year, while in the south it would be used much more. That's why you can't just arbitrarily use a figure. The life should be estimated on the basis of similar property used in your vicinity in a similar business.

Some Final Suggestions

You need to consider carefully the manner in which depreciation of your business assets are being carried on the books. Look behind every figure. Are all the depreciation items listed? Are your policies realistic? Is the length of life right? (You may be carrying items at a much longer length of life than they actually should be.) It is easy to be misled into thinking that these depreciation items are all carefully computed down to the last cent. Analyze each account. Accountants are not as familiar with the motel business as the owners. You must advise as to the usefulness of the property. The accounts then will accurately reflect these costs.

Study some good references. The publication *Tax Guide for Small Business* is excellent. It can be obtained from any office of the Internal Revenue Service for about 40 cents. Read this carefully each year to see where you may be missing some important aspect of your deductible expenses.

Keep up to date. The new additional first-year depreciation allowance for tangible personal property (not buildings) was recently enacted. Designed to aid small business, this extra allowance provides for a straight 20 per cent depreciation the first year *in addition* to the regular depreciation allowance. The property must be purchased after 1957 and is limited to $20,000. Expected life must be six years or more. The property can be new or used. You must recognize, however, that this provision merely speeds up depreciation in the early years and later the allowance will be less. Then there will be a smaller amount of property "on the books" and your depreciation expense will be lower. Total expenses thus will tend to be lower, raising net profit and increasing your income tax liability.

OTHER TAXES

Federal Social Security Taxes

This is a tax imposed jointly on the employer and the employee. The motel's share of the tax is deductible as a business expense. You must collect and pay this tax regardless of the number of employees.

Self-Employment Tax (Social Security)

An owner of a business must pay this tax on the first $4,800 of net earnings. An income of $400 or more is necessary to come under this aspect of the Social Security Tax.

Withholding Tax

You, as an employer, are required to withhold federal income taxes from your employee's pay according to the proper tax schedule. This entire tax is paid by the employee.

Federal Excise Tax

If you have a gift/curio shop and sell jewelry, toilet preparations, leather items, etc., you must collect this tax from the customers.

Federal Unemployment Tax

If you have four or more employees who work at least some portion of one day each of 20 or more calendar weeks during the calendar year, you are liable for this tax. Credit is given for state contributions so that most employers pay a federal unemployment tax of 3/10 of 1 per cent. It is paid by the employer, not the employee.

State Unemployment Tax

Similar rules concerning number of employees and length of work apply to the state tax. Obtain instructions from the state unemployment department.

State Income Tax, Corporation, or Business Taxes

Your state may have these or similar taxes. If so, complete information can be obtained from your accountant or lawyer and from the state tax department.

Sales and Room Taxes

Many states have enacted such taxes. They are charged to the guest, but the motel is responsible as a collecting agent and must transmit the tax to the state. Careful records of the taxes collected is mandatory.

Real Estate and Personal Property Taxes

These taxes are levied by local units of government and are based upon the assessed valuation of the property. An advanced estimate of the taxes can sometimes be obtained when the project is in the blueprint stage. This is very helpful in making up a budget for the new business. Downtown locations usually have higher taxes than suburban or rural locations. This factor must be considered in choosing a location.

As of the publication date of this book, no new taxes have been reported. Only time will tell the story of any additional taxes by various levels of government.

INNKEEPER'S LAWS

Any business which holds forth as a public hostelry offering rooms to the traveling public is subject to a group of laws known as "innkeeper's or hotel laws." Legal application of these laws to the motel field is well established as the laws are customarily written to cover "hotels and similar types of lodging accommodations." The motel manager therefore should understand that the innkeeper's laws of his state apply to his motel. This is in conformance with common law principle that hotel, inn, and motel are synonymous.

Your attorney will be of great assistance in avoiding legal entanglements. Consult him early in the life of the business, preferably when the motel is in the planning stage.

Two Kinds of Law

Laws pertaining to innkeepers are made up of two components—common law and statutory law. There are three principal points covered by both statutory and common law. These points form the background of the law protecting the innkeeper and are the basis of all statutory regulation of motels in the United States. They are: 1) the liability of the innkeeper for the goods of his guests, 2) the lien that the innkeeper has on the property of his guest, and 3) the protection afforded the innkeeper against fraud by the action of the guest. These three points are established in the common and statutory laws of the 50 states.

The Principal Laws and Regulations

Here are the principal categories of innkeeper's laws:

DUTIES AND LIABILITIES OF INNKEEPERS

Liability
Money, jewelry, valuable papers
Liability to person of guests
Civil rights
Unlawful to bar a soldier or sailor
Motel's right of lien and method of enforcement
Unclaimed property
Protection of motel from fraud
Bad check law
Breaking and entering
Fire negligence

REGULATION, OPERATION AND INSPECTION

Equipment necessary in motel buildings more than two stories in height
Equipment necessary in motel buildings not over two stories in height
Sanitation
Towels and bedding
Health regulations
Regulations governing employment of labor
Workmen's compensation
Fair Employment Practices Act
Regulations concerning elevators
Liquor laws

An interesting book of hotel law cases by Hendrick Zwarensteyn, Professor of Hotel and Business Law at Michigan State University, is now available from the Bureau of Business and Economic Research, Eppley Center, Michigan State University, East Lansing. Another book on hotel law is *Fundamentals of Hotel Law,* by Professor Zwarensteyn. This book is recommended for your library also.

CHAPTER 17

Insurance

Insurance is important because it helps protect your assets from many hazards. Probably the most significant is the public liability aspect; savings can be made in fire insurance also. In planning a new motel, certain noncombustible materials and methods used in construction will materially lower the future cost of fire insurance. An example is the use of concrete instead of wood. A concrete roof will carry a lower rate than a wood or asphalt roof.

Serious or even disastrous effects can be experienced by a successful business enterprise from fires, liability suits, or other perils. Counsel from a competent insurance agent is the most practical way to obtain information regarding the essential protection. After selecting a dependable insurance agent, have him make a complete survey of the contingencies which might arise in your business. Then go over this list, selecting the coverages which are needed and which the business can afford.

The newest concept in motel insurance is the so-called "package" motel policy which covers a large number of essential aspects in one special motel policy. Ads for companies writing this coverage appear in the motel trade journals. Your state insurance department can also help locate such companies.

CASUALTY INSURANCE PROTECTION[1]

for

Hotel, Motel, Restaurant or Resort Owners or Operators
All Exposures or Hazards other than
Fire and Allied Coverages

I   Introduction

ESSENTIAL

A. Common law responsibility to the public for the operation of
your business, including all incidental operations. (Legal liability
for bodily injury and/or damage to the property of others.
Liability for personal activities of yourself and members of your
household (not business pursuits).
Liability for injuries to your employees.
Medical payments for injuries to employees and members of the
public (customers, guests, tradesmen, etc.).

IMPORTANT

B. Direct financial loss of money or property, both business and personal, including incidental damage to property.

ADVISABLE

C. Additional possibilities of loss for which you may or may not care
to assume the calculated risk.

II   Normal Hazards Which Create Exposure to Liability

A. Alterations or new construction work by employees or independent
contractors.
B. Automobiles—maintenance, operation or use of hired or owned
cars; or employee owned automobiles, operated for your business.
C. Business premises and all incidental operations and premises.
D. Contractural obligations (hold harmless agreements).
D. Elevators—ownership, maintenance, operation or use.
F. Employees—injuries to themselves or cause injuries to others.
G. False arrest, invasion of privacy.
H. Innkeeper's liability.
I. Personal liability—residence, personal activities.
J. Products—distribution, handling, or sale.

---

[1]Prepared by W. E. Hunt, assistant vice-president, Wolverine Insurance Company,
Battle Creek, Michigan.

Additional hazards which create liability:

Beauty Parlors (malpractice)
Cabins
Canoes or Rowboats
Cottages
Docks or Floats
Drive-ins
Gasoline Stations
Gift or Novelty Shops
Golf Courses
Outboard motors—rented to
    customers
Parking Lots
Physicians (Malpractice)
Playgrounds
Saddle horses
Swimming Beaches
Swimming Pools
Trailer Courts

III Possibilities of Direct Financial Loss of Your Own Property Both Business and Personal

A. Acceptance of counterfeit U.S. paper currency.
B. Automobile loss or damage.
C. Boiler explosion.
D. Burglary or Robbery of money, securities or other property from the business premises or your own residence.
E. Burglary or Robbery away from the premises or residence including loss from the home of a custodian or messenger; or bank depository.
F. Damage to property caused by burglary or attempt thereat.
G. Dishonesty of or embezzlement by an employee.
H. Elevator collision.

IV Additional Possibilities of Losses Which May Be Calculated

A. Loss or damage to neon signs.
B. Loss or damage to plate glass in buildings.

V Essential Protection for Survival

A. Legal liability insurance coverages available for protection against the exposures or hazards enumerated:

Exposures or Hazards	*Kind of Insurance*
1. Alterations or new construction work:	
a. Performed by employees	Manufacturers & Contractors' Liability and Property Damage
b. Performed by independent contractors	Owners'-Contractors' Protective Liability and Property Damage

Exposures or Hazards	*Kind of Insurance*
2. Automobiles:	
a. Owned	Automobile Bodily Injury and Property Damage
b. Employee owned— used in your business	Automobile non-ownership Bodily Injury Liability and Property Damage
c. Hired or Rented	Automobile hired car Bodily Injury Liability and Property Damage
3. Business premises and all incidental operations	Comprehensive Bodily Injury Liability and Property Damage
4. Contractual obligations by written agreement:	
a. Easements	
b. Lease of Premises	Contractural Bodily Injury
c. Marquees	Liability and Property Damage
d. Sidewalk elevators	
e. Signs	

Exposures and Hazards	*Kind of Insurance*
5. Elevators:	
a. Leased and operated by you	
	Elevator Bodily Injury Liability and Property Damage
b. Owned and operated by you	
6. Employees:	
a. Less than three (3) (not subject to Mich. Workmen's Compensation Law)	Employers' Liability and Employees' Medical Payments
b. Three (3) or more (Mich. Workmen's Compensation insurance compulsory)	Workmen's Compensation including Employers' Liability
7. False arrest, invasion of privacy, etc.	False Arrest Liability
8. Innkeeper's liability	Innkeeper's Legal Liability

9. Personal Liability:

a. Residence—Personal activities	Comprehensive Personal Liability—includes personal activities of Insured and members of Insured's household
b. Medical Payments— servants and public	Property Damage and Medical Payments

10. Products — Products Bodily Injury Liability and Property Damage

VI Important Protection Against Direct Financial Loss

A. First Party insurance to protect your property:

Property	*Kind of Insurance*
1. Automobiles—damage, destruction, or theft	Automobile Comprensive and Collision
2. Boilers:	
a. Damage to boilers by explosion	
	Boiler Coverage
b. Resultant damage to your property	
c. Damage to property of others	insured under liability policies in V 3.
3. Burglary, Robbery, Theft or Larceny:	
a. Business fund and property in premises	Broad Form Storekeepers' Burglary; Open Stock Burglary; Money & Securities Broad Form
b. Business funds and property away from premises	Dishonesty, Disappearance and Destruction
c. Personal funds and property in residence	
	Broad Form Personal Theft
d. Personal funds and property away from residence	

4. Dishonesty of employees:
   a. Alteration of bank deposits, checks or forgery
      Check Alteration
      Forgery in 3D

      Depositors Forgery Bond or

   b. Embezzlement

      Individual Fidelity Bond;
      Commercial Blanket Bond;
      Blanket Position Bond

   c. Theft of property
5. Elevators:
   a. Damage to car and equipment

      Elevator Collision

   b. Damage to other property in the elevator, or in your care, custody and control

VII   Advisable Protection for Calculated Losses

A. First party insurance to protect your property:

Property	*Kind of Insurance*
1. Counterfeit U.S. paper currency	Counterfeit Money
2. Loss or damage to Neon Signs	All Risk Neon Sign
3. Plate Glass	Comprehensive Glass

VIII   Summary

A. Foundation of financial security for survival is complete insurance protection against all legal liability claims

Legal Liability Claims	*Kind of Insurance*
1. Counsel or legal fees	Automobile Liability; Comprehensive Business Liability;
2. Court costs	Employers' Liability False Arrest Liability;
3. Judgments	Innkeeper's Liability Personal Liability;
4. Penalties	Workmen's Compensation

NO ESTIMATE OR FORECAST OF THESE LOSSES CAN BE MADE

B. Direct Financial Losses covered by insurance further strengthens the foundation by protection of:

Direct Financial Loss	Kinds Of Insurance
1. Physical Property	Automobile Physical Damage
a. Automobile	
b. Buildings	Burglary
c. Contents (including boilers)	
d. Personal Property	Dishonesty of Employees
	Extended Coverage
2. Income	Fire and Lightning
a. Earnings	Inland Marine
b. Profits	Medical Payments
c. Rents	Personal Theft

CHAPTER 18

Housekeeping and Maintenance

Probably the most loosely organized aspect of motel management is in the area of housekeeping and maintenance. Yet, this often requires the greatest expenditure of labor and operating expense and certainly means much to the success of the motel. No matter whether the motel is small or large, bathrooms must be cleaned, rooms must be made up, and equipment must be maintained. Modern motel guests demand very high standards of housekeeping and maintenance. It is up to management to supply them.

HOUSEKEEPING

A first obligation of management is to hire a competent executive housekeeper. This person (even if the wife of the manager) must have the following qualifications:

—One who has all the normal qualifications of a good employee: cooperative; dependable; honest; can communicate; leadership ability; enthusiastic; pleasing personality.

—One who is competent in the technical aspects of her job: knows about materials of construction and their upkeep; knows how to judge quality of supplies; knows how to judge cleaning and maintenance equipment; knows basic procedures for all housekeeping.

—One who has had experience and is adaptable to the policies of the house; can adjust to type of trade; has demonstrated that she knows her job.

Duties of the executive or head housekeeper include:

1. Keeping the front office informed of rooms as they are ready for occupancy by new guests.

2. Hiring and supervising the work of the maids, and sometimes of yardman and porter.

3. Assigning rooms to be cleaned and other duties to the maids.

4. Keeping an accurate count of the linen that is sent to the laundry and of the clean linen as it is returned. If linen rental is used, then similar counts and checks should be made. (This is not necessary if the motel has its own laundry.)

5. Supervising and helping in redecorating and rehabilitating the rooms and furnishings.

6. Purchasing housekeeping supplies and linens after consultation with the manager.

7. Notifying the manager of rooms out of order and needing repair or other special attention.

Determine Requirements

Before staff can be organized, budgets established, or housekeeping work started, an inventory of areas to be maintained must be made. First, determine the categories of the areas to be serviced: guest rooms, lobby, corridors, dining rooms, bars and cocktail lounges, conference rooms, etc. Next, what is the area of each? Next the frequency of maintenance must be determined, which of course depends upon the standards of maintenance desired, the nature of the construction materials, and the amount of traffic. At this point it is well to decide how much of the maintenance will be done by employees of the motel and how much will be contracted out. This depends a great deal upon the availability of contract work in the vicinity of the motel and comparisons of costs. Most motels consider it to their advantage to have daily room cleaning and make-up done by their own staff while laundry, painting, and room repair are often contracted out.

After this, management should be able to determine the number of workers for each type of duty. The following tables should be helpful.

STANDARD JOB TIME LIST [1]

	Time in Seconds		Time in Seconds
DUSTING		Sand Urns	60
Ash Tray	15	Spittoons	180
Book Cases		Tables	
13" x 35" x 12"	22	Large	60
36" x 30" x 8"	33	Medium	35
12' x 40" x 12"	216	Small	22
42" x 24" x 11"	49	Telephone	9
Cabinets		Typewriter (Covered)	7
36" x 77" x 18"	106	Vending Machine	60
30" x 66" x 18"	42	Venetian Blinds (Standard)	210
Calculators		Wastebaskets	15
Small	7		
Large	9	**LAVATORY ITEMS**	
Chairs		Cleaning Commode	
Large	63	(With Partitions)	180
Medium	35	Door (Spot Wash)	50
Steno	22	Door Latch	10
Cigarette Stand	25	Mirrors	
Clock, Desk	8	25" x 49"	20
Clock, Wall	20	60" x 21"	20
Desks		88" x 31"	40
Large	48	Napkin Dispenser	13
Medium	43	Napkin Disposal	10
Small	38	Paper Towel Dispenser	7
Desk Items, Misc.	3	Paper Towel Disposal	10
Doors		Shelving	
Without glass	25	20" long	8
With glass	40	126" x 6"	60
Elevator Cabs (Inside)	196	Urinals — Complete	120
Files		Wainscoting	
4 drawer	22	75-100 Ft. Long	25
5 drawer	27	Wash Basin, Soap	
Fire Extinguishers	16	Dispenser	120
In and Out Trays	8		
Lamps and Lights		**WASHING**	
Wall Flourescent	8	Glass Partitions	
Desk Flourescent	18	Clear 8 Sq. Ft. Per Min.	
Table Lamp, Shade	35	Opaque 20 Sq. Ft. Per Min.	
Floor Lamp, Shade	35		
Partitions, Glass 50 Sq. Ft.		**MISCELLANEOUS**	
per Minute		Door (Washing)	150
Rack, Coat and Hat (6)	90	Drinking Fountain	90
Radiators and Window		Vacuuming	
Ledge (124" x 15")	45	Large Divan	190
Radiator (Flush with Wall)			
40" x 30" x 6'	21		

NOTE:

Indicates average working times of skilled workers operating under average conditions. Since conditions vary in every building, use only as a guide in planning cleaning work assignments.

---

[1] From *BUILDINGS*, November, 1960

STANDARD JOB TIMES FOR FLOOR CLEANING OPERATIONS[2]
Time in Minutes per 1,000 Sq. Ft.

SWEEPING		MACHINE SCRUB	
Unobstructed	9	Unobstructed	25
Slightly Obstructed	10	Slightly Obstructed	35
Obstructed	12	Obstructed	40
Heavily Obstructed	16	Heavily Obstructed	45
DUST MOPPING		MACHINE POLISH	
Unobstructed	7	Unobstructed	15
Slightly Obstructed	9	Slighlty Obstructed	25
Obstructed	12	Obstructed	30
Heavily Obstructed	16	Heavily Obstructed	35
DAMP MOPPING		VACUUM—WET PICK-UP	
Unobstructed	16	Unobstructed	20
Slightly Obstructed	23	Slightly Obstructed	27
Obstructed	27	Obstructed	31
Heavily Obstructed	32	Heavily Obstructed	35
WET MOP AND RINSE		VACUUM—DRY PICK-UP	
Unobstructed	35	Unobstructed	14
Slightly Obstructed	45	Slightly Obstructed	17
Obstructed	50	Obstructed	19
Heavily Obstructed	55	Heavily Obstructed	23
HAND SCRUB		STRIP AND REWAX	
Unobstructed	240	Unobstructed	100
Slightly Obstructed	300	Slightly Obstructed	120
Obstructed	330	Obstructed	140
Heavily Obstructed	360	Heavily Obstructed	180
HAND SCRUB—LONG BRUSH		COMBINATION SCRUBBER	
Unobstructed	75	5,000 to 20,000	
Slightly Obstructed	105	Sq. Ft. per Hour	
Obstructed	120		
Heavily Obstructed	135		

Organization of Manpower

At the start, even in a small motel, every person should know his position in the organization. To whom is he responsible? The popular method is to set up an organization chart—desirable even with only a few employees. This helps to avoid misunderstandings and is absolutely essential in larger organizations.

The function of each job should be clear. The jurisdiction, the duties, the relationships with other employees, the limits of authority, the objectives and how performance will be measured are the responsibility of management right at the start.

With this, the executive housekeeper can set up a budget. Generally, about 1/4 of gross room sales is needed by the housekeeping department for salaries, wages, laundry, linen, and other expenses. It is extremely important that good records be kept by the housekeeping department. Only in this way can top management know the relationship

---

[2]From *BUILDINGS*, November, 1960

MAINTENANCE COSTS FOR CARPETED AND NON-CARPETED FLOORS[3]

| | LIGHT Conditions of Soil | | | MEDIUM Conditions of Soil | | | HEAVY Conditions of Soil | | |
	Minute per 1000 sq. ft.	Annual Cost of Individual Operations per 1000 sq. ft. Carpet	Non Carpet	Minute per 1000 sq. ft.	Annual Cost of Individual Operations per 1000 sq. ft. Carpet	Non Carpet	Minute per 1000 sq. ft.	Annual Cost of Individual Operations per 1000 sq. ft. Carpet	Non Carpet
DAILY									
Vacuum	12	$ 65.00		18	$ 97.50		24	$130.00	
Dust Mop	9		$ 48.75	11		$ 59.60	15		$ 81.25
Buff	12		65.00	18		97.50	24		130.00
WEEKLY									
Spot clean	24	26.00		30	32.50		36	39.00	
Wet mop	18		19.50	24		26.00	48		52.00
BI-MONTHLY									
Refinish	180		22.50	240		30.00			
MONTHLY									
Refinish							300		75.00
SEMI-ANNUALLY									
Complete shampoo							240	10.00	
ANNUAL									
Traffic area shampoo	180	1.90		240	2.50				
Complete shampoo	180	3.80		240	5.00				
Total Labor Cost		96.70	155.75		137.50	213.10		179.00	338.25
Supplies Cost		7.00	24.60		8.00	30.00		10.00	45.00
Total Annual Maintenance Cost for all operations per 1000 sq. ft.		104.00	180.00		146.00	243.00		189.00	383.00

Labor costs are based on an hourly wage rate of $1.25. Service is assumed to be 5 days a week, or 260 days a year. Time rates for each maintenance operation are based on careful studies of each operation.

To arrive at an annual cost for each operation:
>   multiply the time required (converted to hours), times $1.25 times 260 days.

For example, in areas of heavy soil:
1.   Daily vacuuming takes 24 minutes, or 2/5 of an hour:
>   2/5 x $1.25 = $.50 per day. $.50 x 260 = $130.00 annual vacuuming cost.

2.   Weekly spot cleaning takes 36 minutes or 3/5 of an hour:
>   3/5 x $1.25 = $.75. $.75 x 52 = $39.00

3.   Monthly refinishing takes 300 minutes or 5 hours:
>   5 x $1.25 = $6.25 $6.25 x 12 = $75.00.

4.   Shampooing. In areas of heavy congestion and soil the entire carpeted area is shampooed twice a year. Thus in areas of heavy soil the annual shampooing cost is shown at $10.00.
>   240 minutes = 4 hours x $1.25 = $5.00 x 2 = $10.00.

>   In areas of medium and light conditions of soil and congestion, carpeted areas require one complete shampooing a year plus one shampooing of traffic areas only. Traffic areas cover only approximately 50% of the total area and are so designated because they are the most affected by soil and congestion.

5.   Total Annual Maintenance Costs are quoted in round figures, i.e., to the nearest dollar.

[3] From *BUILDINGS,* November, 1960

of sales to costs and the possible need for making changes in the establishment, the staff, or methods.

Forecasting

An extremely difficult but important chore is determining the daily, weekly, and monthly needs of manpower and supplies. This takes experience and judgement and of course, good records. Close contact with the reservations clerk is essential to know when peaks or lows of demand are coming. Examination of past records is helpful to learn of regular or seasonal changes. Policies vary, with some motels maintaining a full staff of maids at all times, giving them special room cleaning duties during low occupancy, others maintain a minimum core staff with several part-time maids on call when the demand appears. No matter how it is done, every room must be in rentable order just as soon as possible after it has been vacated, and at no time should any guest be shown a room which is not absolutely completely ready for occupancy.

The Daily Room Report

Larger motels should require the housekeepers to hand in a Daily Room Report at the beginning of their work shift. The report goes to either the housekeeper or directly to the front office, depending upon motel policy. Sometimes duplicates are made, the original going to the front office, the carbon copy to the housekeeper.

The report itself may be simple. Sometimes a small scratch pad is used. The housekeeper merely lists the room numbers of rooms still occupied, rooms occupied but which will be ready for new occupancy, rooms that were vacant, and rooms out of order.

A simple mimeographed form such as the one illustrated next can be used:

The best practice is to have all rooms made up and ready for occupancy by about 3:00 P.M. Where you have late check-outs or day rentals, an afternoon and evening housekeeper will be needed.

As each room is made up and ready for occupancy, the housekeeper calls the front desk on the phone, reporting on the room. This practice keeps the front desk fully informed as to the rentability of each room. We recommend this practice.

Selection and Training

While top management has the over-all responsibility for all employee recruitment, it usually falls upon the executive housekeeper to

DAILY ROOM REPORT
KEY

| / Room still occupied | Vacant |
| x Slept in, guests departed | o Out of order |

```
1/    2/    3x    4x    5    6∅    7/    8x    9x    10x
11/   12/   13/   14/   15x   16∅   17x   18x   19x   20∅
21/   22/   23/   24x   25/   26∅   27/   28x   29x   30∅
31x   32x   33x   34    35x
```

o...o

Comments:

    5 face towels used
    24 basin drain clogged

                    Signed: M. Smith

o...o

ROOMS:	CONDITION:
1-2-6-7-11-12-13-14-16	Still occupied
20-21-22-23-25-26-27-30	
3-4-8-9-10-15-17-18-19	Slept in, guests
28-29-31-32-33-35	departed
5-34	Vacant
24	Out of order

hire and train her employees. Depending upon the labor market, advertising for help may or may not be necessary. Many motels have a waiting list of applicants. In any case, some entrance test should be given and an interview held to determine whether or not the applicant can do the work expected of her.

Generally, three methods of training are popular throughout moteldom: "sink-or-swim;" on-the-job training; and classroom instruction. In the first, no training is given—the maid is put right onto the job. Although frequently practiced, nothing good can be said about this method. It assumes that the maid is well trained, which she often is not. Even though she may have had experience elsewhere, there is much to teach her about the specific policies and nature of a certain motel. The second method is most popular and brings good results. A supervisor outlines the procedures to the maid and at the same time shows her how to do them. The last method is practiced in larger establishments where film, text, or lecture methods are used to save time. This method is effective only when combined with actually doing the task. See Chapter 13.

Selection of Cleaners and Waxes

One of the most difficult tasks is choosing and purchasing the correct materials for cleaning and waxing. Each advertiser extolls his brand as the best for motel use but most housekeepers prefer the trial-and-error method. Any reputable supplier should not object to providing samples for testing in the motel with its own labor and cleaning equipment. Not only is much money wasted on poor cleaners but often permanent damage is done to fine fixtures and surfaces. A good cleaner should:

> Do an effective job of cleaning the soil
> Leave little or no film
> Be safe to use, both for worker and for the
> surface

As more carpeting is used, less area is waxed, but wherever waxed floors are desired, the selection of a good floor wax poses no serious problem today.

Furniture Cleaning and Repair

Most motels today find it much to their advantage to contract out the maintenance of furnishings. Only in larger establishments or those remotely located where such services are unavailable does it pay to maintain such specialized staff.

Selection of Linens and Mattresses

The choice of linens generally depends upon weighing several factors and then making a decision. Most important of these factors are:

> Durability
> Laundry cost
> Purchase price
> Type of motel

Striped, plain or flowered sheets in colors may be suited to certain operations but plain white is preferred by most guests, especially men. The higher the class of the business, the higher the quality of the sheet must be. Percale sheets with thread count of 180 are preferred by many but experts call attention to tensile strength as a better measure of durability. We should remember, however, that the greatest wear of sheets in motels is generally caused by misuse or abuse by either the guests or maids. Only one who has specialized in the purchase of linens should attempt to buy them.

The selection of mattresses is complicated by changes in tastes of the guests. It goes without saying that all mattresses should provide sleeping comfort and the only real test is to lie on one. A compromise must be struck somewhere between the softest and the most firm—recent guest trends have been toward the firmer mattresses.

Laundry Considerations

In many cases laundry can be done more cheaply with relatively inexperienced help on the motel premise. In others, it may be better management to rent uniforms and all linens, taking advantage of the specialized knowledge, high efficiency and mass purchasing power of the contract laundryman.

A laundry-cost survey in fifteen Florida towns and cities showed that the cost of laundry involved in a daily room change varied from twenty cents to sixty-eight cents. In other words, commercial laundries in some places charged almost three and one-half times as much as in other places. The average daily change for a twin bedroom comprised 16 pieces: 4 sheets, 2 pillow cases, 4 bath towels, and 6 face towels.

L. A. Bradley, laundry consultant for the American Hotel and Motel Association, recommends considering your own motel laundry installation whenever commercial laundry costs reach 6 cents a pound, or $3.00 per 100 pounds. Mr. Bradley states that it costs about $100 per room to install a laundry in hotels not exceeding 200 rooms.

A motel laundry has these possible advantages over contracting the laundry: better control over the washing process; better inventory control; better availability of clean linens. A tax advantage also exists in that laundry equipment can be depreciated at 10 per cent a year.

Many motels turned to rental linens when they found that the convenience and absence of investment made this method the best. Your decision must rest upon an examination of the three methods—own and do your own linens, own your linens and send to a laundry, or rent linens. Whichever is cheapest and maintains high quality and service is the best—it's as simple as that. Keep in mind that even if you rent linens you will still need some laundry equipment for miscellaneous washing jobs—usually towels, spreads, drapes, etc.

Room Make-Up and Cleaning

Opinions vary, but many motel men prefer one maid per room rather than two: reduces wasted time in conversation; narrows down responsibility; induces pride in accomplishment. Depending upon the size of room and quality of upkeep, one maid can clean and make-up from ten to sixteen rooms in a full day's work. The lower figure would indicate deluxe rooms and demanding standards of maintenance; the higher would suggest smaller rooms, fewer fixtures, and beyond that number would invite poorer standards of upkeep.

The best system, in the opinion of many, is to maintain a central storage room for all cleaning supplies and to stock maids' carts daily from this center. This allows complete control of supplies, requires fewer maids' rooms scattered throughout the building, and improves the efficiency of the housekeeping department.

The techniques of room make-up and cleaning vary from motel to motel and more is to be learned from the experienced supervisor or housekeeper than from books.

How to Make a Bed—A Time-Saving Method

Most of us make a bed by putting on the first sheet, tucking it in on the sides and mitering it on the corners at the foot of the bed. We repeat this with the second sheet, the blanket and the spread. Each piece of linen requires that we walk around the bed at least once. Time for this method was 5 minutes, 32 seconds.

The new way for making beds entails but one and three-quarters trip around the bed. The major difference between the old and new methods is that all of the linen is placed on the bed at once, all adjusted at one time at each of the four corners of the bed. The head is made completely before anything is done to the foot.

The sequence of steps is as follows:

1. Standing at the left head of the bed the maid spreads the bottom sheet and tucks it in for the few feet closest to her. The sheet can be thrown to cover the bed and the maid does not leave her position to adjust the sheet at other corners.

   a. Remaining in the same spot, she spreads the top sheet, but does not tuck it in. Tucking in the top sheet takes time and is unnecessary.

    b. The blanket is spread and adjusted in the same manner.

    c. The spread is thrown and adjusted.

    d. A pillow is picked up from the opposite side of the bed, encased, folded, and spotted in its correct place.

2. Next the maid walks to the foot of the bed nearest her last standing position and miters the sheets and adjusts the blanket and spread.

3. The next step comprises doing step 2 at the other foot of the bed.

4. Lastly the maid walks around to the other side of the head of the bed and repeats these five steps, adjusting the sheets, blanket, spread and pillow.

In the research study the old way took 5 minutes and 32 seconds. The old method was well established in the maid's habit-system. The new way which was done without training and the establishment of habits took 4 minutes 29 seconds—or a reduction of 63 seconds and at least four trips around the bed.

MAINTENANCE

Probably of least concern to the guest but of vital importance to success of any motel is the maintenance of the establishment. In small motels of the past, this was the responsibility of the owner-manager who often was his own handyman. In modern motels of 100 or more rooms, there is a full-time person in charge of maintenance staff.

As in the housekeeping department, the maintenance department should be properly organized, staffed, and have clearly defined duties and responsibilities.[4] Generally, the types of work included are:

—Electrical

    Maintenance of electrical system

    Maintenance of motors

    Electrical appliances for meetings and conventions

    Radio, TV and communication systems

—Plumbing

    Maintenance of water supply, plumbing fixtures

    Maintenance of sewage system

    Maintenance of wet heating system

---

[4] For further information, see: *Maintenance and Engineering*, by Frank Borsenik, and *Manual for Supervising Housekeeping* by Jean Kimball, both published by the American Hotel and Motel Association Educational Institute, Michigan State University, East Lansing, Michgan.

—Heating, Ventilating and Air Conditioning

Maintenance of all heating, ventilating and air conditioning systems

—General Repair and Maintenance

Structural maintenance
Care of departmental tools, supplies, equipment
Care of grounds

—Fire Prevention and Protection

CHAPTER 19

Public Relations
and Hospitality

What is Public Relations?

The favorable acceptance of your business by the public is of utmost importance. No business is more concerned with human relations than the public hospitality industry—motels, resorts, hotels and restaurants. We are concerned not only with good public relations outside our walls but with having smooth and harmonious relations with our managers and our employees.

Public relations can be defined as an attitude of management which places first priority on the public interest when making any management decisions. In other words, the manager of the business tries *first* to produce satisfactions for his public—guests, employees, owners, neighbors and the whole community. Public relations is a "social conscience" which permeates the entire organization.

An important responsibility of the manager is to create conditions within the business which are conducive to social well-being and then to vigorously relate these conditions to the public—to tell everyone what a fine motel is being operated in his community.

Achieving Good Public Relations

All of the public interests must be served. Serving one group of the public at the expense of another would be very poor all the way around and would not produce desirable public relations.

Good morals are essential to sound public opinion. Each individual business manager and the business he represents must be respected and earn the confidence of his community. There is no difference between his personal reputation and the reputation of his business. They are both earned in the same way.

Favorable public relations with employees emphasizes respect for personality and human dignity. Workers need to have opportunities for self-expression, to help make decisions affecting their interests, and to have a reasonable amount of security.

Your employees have a powerful influence on the public also, as *they represent you* in the public's viewpoint. Teach your employees to be courteous, respectful and always helpful to guests. Little things make a big difference and the attitude of your employees can make or break good public relations.

In formulating any type of management policy, consider initially the possible public reaction to such policy. Weigh this carefully before putting the policy into effect.

For example, you may decide to raise your rates. How will this affect your present clientele? New guests? Your future market for business? New or untried markets?

Likewise, you need to know the attitude of the public towards your present policies. Ask some of your guests as a sample. Perhaps you might learn that they think your rates are too low for the value they receive!

Communication is the lifeblood of good public relations. One interpretation of this concept is to *do good things and then tell the public about it.*

Every motel and resort needs to acquaint the public with factual information about the business. False information, rumors, and gossip are detrimental. Don't fail to communicate the actual conditions as they exist at your place of business. People are curious anyway and *want* to know more about what's going on in their community.

Suppose you, as manager, are to participate in an educational short course at your state university. An item about this in your local newspaper will build goodwill and respect for your business. Or you might serve as host to a community chest group by giving a lawn party. This should be covered by the press with a story and possibly pictures of the event. There also are possibilities for personal communication, radio, and even television.

Developing Favorable Public Impressions

In a sense, good public relations is goodwill. The best public relations specialist in the world cannot do a thing for you unless you first instigate the things that are right for you.

Public service is something you give—your time or talents, your hospitality—and you reap the rewards. Both advertising and public relations will pay for themselves many times over. If you are a small organization and cannot hire public relations help, at least get their advice.

If you are going to try a do-it-yourself program, start with a public service contribution as before mentioned. A party for retarded children or similar good cause is a possibility. If you are a good host, hold a press party to announce some new construction, expansion, or other newsworthy event. Again, this will certainly be of great benefit to you.

Sometimes a new owner will find that his place has a poor reputation and he needs a positive, favorable public relations program to wipe out the unfavorable public impression. A careful review of the recommended procedures outlined in this section should suggest many avenues to achieving good public relations.

You need continuing publicity over the years. There are countless ways of getting publicity, but don't overdo it. There are three guides to remember: planning, propriety, and a sense of rules.

Publicity is just a part of public relations. What you do and how you do it is most important.

Your standards of cleanliness and maintenance, together with a program of accident prevention, can help assure the good reputation of the business. Carelessness along these lines can undo the work of many years and the large amount of money invested in the business.

The rewards of an imaginative and vigorous public relations program will be to establish your business as a valuable and wholesome influence in the community. The public and your guests will recognize your business as one which gives *welcome employment* and *provides its guests and customers with the most satisfying of services and products* which are *good values* for the *rates and prices charged.*

THE ART OF HOSPITALITY

The "big three" of motel management are attractive and comfortable facilities, cleanliness, and *hospitality.* Consider carefully this matter of hospitality and how you can make this element of your business outstanding. If you can make your guests feel *happy* and *important,* they will come back again and enthusiastically recommend your place to their friends.

Hospitality is of the spirit—intangible—yet it is a vital ingredient of success. It is an art which must be constantly practiced in order to achieve and maintain a high level of proficiency. Once you have the true spirit of hospitality you can never lose it. Like playing the piano, the more you work at it the better you become.

Letters and Printed Material

Hospitality begins in your letters to prospective guests. Are you original? Do you use your imagination to create distinctive letterheads, envelopes, folders and other literature? These printed pieces should be fresh, colorful, inviting—and practically "smile" at your guests. They should give them the impression "my! that motel must be a very nice friendly place."

Begin each letter in a friendly way and then put the business part in the middle. A hand written postscript helps to personalize letters.

Signs

Signs likewise should radiate friendliness and hospitality. The impression received by the traveler as he reads your sign will strongly influence him. Whether this influence is good or bad will depend on how the sign is worded. Select phrases such as "Welcome" or "Traditional Hospitality" or similar expressions. This will make the guest feel as though you welcome his business and want him to stop.

Greeting

Dignity and ethics in this industry favor the system whereby the prospective guest leaves his car and walks into the office of the motel. Having the motel manager greet the prospective at his car is not recommended. It puts the motel owner at a disadvantage and encourages bargaining and "shopping." Maintain your front office and lobby in a neat, attractive manner. This will create a favorable impression on the guest. As he approaches the desk, smile and say "good afternoon or good evening." Offering to shake hands and giving your name as manager is good practice if the situation is such that this can be done in a relaxed, informal manner. The big advantage of this practice is that you learn the prospective guest's name and can then use it in your conversation with him. You then ask how many persons are in the party and proceed to sell an appropriate room.

Referrals

In case you do not have a suitable room, always offer to find one for the party. Make calls to other good motels or hotels. When a room has been located, use a simplified map to show how to reach the new place. A folder of your place which includes a map of the community and its environs is one of the handiest and most appreciated items you can provide your guests and prospective guests.

"Package Vacation Concept"

Your guests want more than shelter. If you do not have food service, recommend good eating places. Entertainment and sightseeing suggestions are also appreciated. Vacationists are very responsive to suggestions concerning places to visit, entertainment, where to see historic spots, wildlife, fishing places and similar activities. Ask them what they would like to see and do while in your community and then tell them what you have to offer. Place pictures of outstanding local tourist attractions on the walls of the office and lobby. Be sure there are captions under each picture which provide information about each point of interest. A rack which displays folders of interest to tourists is also appreciated. You can quite easily obtain literature for these racks and they are helpful to travelers.

Flowers

Nothing is more appealing to the guest than some beautiful flowers in the lobby, dining room and even in guest rooms. Using flowers compliments the guest. Even artificial flowers are better than none. Use them often as an expression of esteem and hospitality.

Getting Acquainted

Helping people get acquainted is good hospitality. In addition to learning their names yourself, you can help make the guests feel at home by introducing them to your staff, your family, and other guests. One very successful manager provides a list of all guests to each housekeeper. If one of these housekeepers should have the opportunity to greet guests, she can do so using the guest's name. This will make a very good impression.

An excellent opportunity for hospitality is provided when showing rooms. During the walk from the office to the room, ask about road conditions, home town, destination and similar matters. This will indicate your sincere interest in the guest's welfare, and will result in friendly and appreciative guests.

CREDIT CARDS

As part of the "buyer's market" motel owners have been prone to provide every conceivable inducement to sell rooms and achieve a high occupancy. One such device is the credit card—actually a sales method which affords a fee to the credit card company and consequently a discount or commission paid by the motel. This discount is therefore a cost of doing business and is classified in the *Uniform Classification of Accounts for Motels, Motor Hotels, and Highway Lodges* as an expense under Commissions, Discounts and Allowances.

Honoring credit cards is somewhat like advertising, as the display of the credit card seal on the lobby window and use of the outdoor sign provide an inducement to the prospective guest to stop. Commissions are paid only on credit sales which are billed through the credit card company. A guest thus may carry a card but pay cash for his room and then no commission would be incurred.

Some of the endorsing and referral organizations require the honoring of cards. If the billing is done through the central office of the referral organization, the percentage of commission paid is reduced—a direct saving as a result of membership.

Honoring credit cards usually results in complicating your bookkeeping system. The Carte Blanche card is unique in that sales made through this system are the same as cash and the motel receives immediate credit to its account when the charge slips are deposited in the bank. The other cards, American Express and Diner's Club, require a period of waiting until the funds are received. Amount of commission paid varies somewhat with the volume of business which is done under some of the credit card plans.

Whether or not to honor the cards is often a difficult decision. Experience to date in the motel field does not seem to warrant the use of the cards. The chain motel organizations are accustomed to honoring cards, but by and large, the motels of the country have not felt that it was necessary. Perhaps increasing competition in the future may force more widespread adoption of the cards, but for the present they are not universally used.

CHAPTER 20

Advertising and Sales Promotion

What is Advertising?

Advertising can be defined as paid public messages designed to tell about or praise your business. These are carried through displays, newspapers, radio or other media.

Advertising is paid for by the business manager for the avowed purpose of profiting from the anticipated increase in business. Effective advertising must gain the attention of the prospective guest, hold his attention for sufficient time to have him appreciate the message, and make a lasting and effective impression on the prospect's mind.

Publicity, in contrast, is favorable information, usually printed, which brings your business to the attention of the public. It is not paid for, but contributed by a public information medium because of its news value.

Both advertising and publicity are conducted by the business in order to make a profit. This is the essence of all private enterprise. Advertising and publicity are universally recognized as normal and desirable aspects of business management.

Importance of Advertising

Every motel needs at least some form of advertising to keep revenues at a level sufficient to produce a profit. In addition to value of word-of-mouth testimonials and endorsements (which are the most valuable of all ways of getting business), a well organized advertising program is considered essential. New customers and guests are constantly needed to insure a level of sales which will be wholly satisfactory to the management and owners.

The Touch of Quality

Like looking in a mirror, the advertising which you do reflects you, your personality, and your business. Because of this, you cannot afford to use anything but the very best to create the most favorable image in the customer's mind.

To most prospective guests, your advertising will be their first introduction to your business. The success of this introduction will depend upon the impression made. To insure that this impression will be favorable, all advertising media should have the touch of quality—a cleanness of form and dignified, convincing messages. A flavor of showmanship is needed in order to make your advertising efforts distinctive, interesting and compelling. There is so much competition that if advertising is to be effective it must stand out as superior to anything else in your vicinity.

PLANNING THE ADVERTISING PROGRAM

Making Your Market Analysis for Advertising

Before you can plan an intelligent and well organized advertising program you need to know some important facts about your prospective guest. In other words, determine your market before deciding on how to reach it.

Market analysis consists of determining: 1) the types or classes of guests you can successfully serve, 2) the geographical areas from which you attract guests (or could attract them), and 3) how much business you could obtain with your present facilities, or what your facilities *could* be through additions or remodeling.

Types of Guests

The first consideration lies in the classes or categories of customers you want. No motel or resort can successfully accommodate everybody. Managers must gear their facilities and services to a somewhat narrow range of price appeals, realizing full well that they cannot provide the type of facilities desired by a wide diversity of guests.

The market for your place must be clearly fixed in your mind. Who are you best qualified to serve? Well-to-do couples? Traveling men? Business executives? Young honeymoon couples? Families in the medium income bracket? Low income families traveling on a budget? Wealthy sportsmen? These are just examples of market groups whose characteristics can be grouped by: 1) income and price class, 2) cultural interests, 3) age, 4) predominant activity such as sports, etc., 5) services desired and 6) length of stay.

Every motel business can probably serve successfully several groups of customers such as commercial travelers and tourists or vacationists and retired couples. The more groups you can accommodate the better, but this definitely has its limitations.

GEOGRAPHICAL AREAS FOR BUSINESS

The second consideration concerns a knowledge of where your business comes from or could come from. By studying your guest registration cards, you can organize this data on a map or by tally. One motel found that 92 per cent of its registered guests came from a radius of 200 miles or less from the motel. Such a study will provide an excellent insight into the geographical locations for the most effective, concentrated advertising.

Don't overlook, however, business from a considerable distance. For example, a Pontiac, Michigan, motel operator has done a good business through travel agents in California, who send the motel business from those who fly to Michigan to pick up new cars.

SIZE OF BUSINESS, AND POTENTIAL

Your share of the market will be determined by the number of rooms and the variety of facilities you offer. For example, if you installed a children's playground, you could expect to serve a wider range of guests than you could without such facility. Likewise, food service and meeting rooms can further widen your market and potential market. Your share of the market therefore can be increased by expanding or remodeling your facility.

TWO MARKET TYPES

Are your prospective guests ending their trip at your place? If so, this market could be called *terminal*. This would be the prevailing type of guest at resorts and resort-type motels.

If you are seeking guests who are passing by, then this would be a *transient* type market. Motels seek this type of guest and actively promote business by roadside signs and other types of advertising.

Prospects in the *terminal* category are:

1. Resort guests and those at resort-atmosphere places which can accommodate week-end guests, or those staying even longer.
2. Business visitors to the community.
3. Residential visitors who can more conveniently sleep in a motel than at their host's home.
4. Attendees at group meetings or conventions.
5. Visitors attracted by special events, tourist attractions, or features such as festivals, tournaments, celebrations, shows, tours, historical sites, games, or fairs.

Prospects in the *transient* category include:

1. Business travelers passing through the community.
2. Vacationers on their way to a terminal point or another destination.

How to Analyze Markets for Advertising

In applying market analysis to advertising, review the characteristics of each market group. Then determine which of these groups you can best serve. Consider also what new and additional groups could be served by remodeling or enlarging your facilities. Perhaps there are entirely new markets which you could develop.

After studying these possibilities, develop an advertising program which will appeal to each of the groups which you deem to be a good prospect.

In regard to your present clientele, you should know the answers to the following questions before a well planned advertising program can be formulated:

1. Where do your guests come from?
2. Why did they come your way—purpose of trip?
3. How long did they stay?

The only really satisfactory method of finding out this information is to *ask the guest personally.* Written questionnaires and other devices seldom produce as good results.

Information obtained by the interview should be carefully tabulated and recorded. If you know a lot about your present guests, then you can devise means of increasing patronage from similar sources.

A statistical device regarding guest information data is to arrange it in *series* or *trends.* For example, the business you got from Chicago last year was 10 per cent of your total business and for the year before it was 15 per cent. This is valuable information. Use it to provide the basis for constructive action through advertising and other means to regain this business.

Think about these questions: Where do *you* fit into the market situation? How do you appeal to your best prospects? What are they seeking? What can be done through advertising? Personal selling? Publicity? Through tourist associations, endorsing and referral organizations? Through travel agents?

Concepts of a Coordinated Program

"Hit or miss" advertising efforts are largely a waste of money. Promotion-wise motel and resort managers make their advertising dollars do double duty. They invest in a multiphase program in which each part strengthens the other. An example is the use of outdoor advertising displays which tie in closely with radio advertising. A motorist hears a radio "commercial" of a motel. Soon he sees the outdoor highway advertising of this same motel. Such a coordinated program can make a much more lasting and effective impression on the mind of the prospective guest than that of an unplanned program. He *heard* the message and then *saw* the outdoor sign.

Planning and coordinating your advertising efforts in this manner is the *only* way you can obtain full effectiveness from advertising expenditures.

Using An Advertising Agency

Motel managers *must* know the fundamentals of marketing, advertising and selling. However, to be an expert in these matters takes specialized skill and experience. The most satisfactory way in which to utilize expert advertising ability is to engage an advertising agency.

The purpose of an advertising agency is to increase your business and do it profitably. An advertising agency—

1. *Works with ideas in copy and in layout.* Copy is the term used to describe written messages. Layout refers to the arrangement of copy, art, and pictures.

2. *Advises on the choice of channels* to convey advertising messages. This involves an organized and carefully worked out plan using newspapers, magazines, radio, TV, guide books, posters, direct mail, postcards, folders, or other advertising media.

3. *Conducts market analysis* to direct advertising intelligently to those who are the best prospects.

4. *Assists in planning and carrying out a publicity and public relations program for the business.*

When seeking the services of an advertising agency, look for successful experience which the agency has had in promoting your type of business. The emphasis should be on the *quality* of the job they can do for you. Check the advertising campaigns they have conducted and ascertain the effect of the agency's work.

Advertising agencies receive a 15 per cent commission from the various media through which the advertising is placed. Also, a usual practice is to charge a fee for copy and layout services. Several arrangements for paying the advertising agency are used. Examples are a fee plus commission, fee minus commission, a flat fee, or a cost-plus fee. Determine in advance the arrangements for paying the agency.

The financial integrity and credit rating of an advertising agency can be checked by contacting art studies, printing companies, or others doing business with the agency. In addition agencies which are members of the American Association of Advertising Agencies are reliable.

Plan your advertising program objectively with specific goals—achievable goals—set forth. Then your advertising agency can assist in achieving the goals.

For single piece printing such as a folder or postcard, a creative printer is often very helpful. For an over-all advertising program, however, the advice of an advertising agency experienced and successful in motel or resort work is most valuable.

Setting the Advertising Budget

After the preliminary planning of an over-all program, the next step is to adjust this program to the funds available. Reappraise your program in light of your goals and then proceed with the high priority essential items.

Promoting a new business will require more money than promotion for one with an established clientele.

No specific amount can be recommended to budget for advertising and sales promotion. This amount will depend on each individual circumstance. Every business is different. Some may find that a very small advertising budget produces satisfactory results. Others might spend 10 per cent of their gross sales or more and profit accordingly.

Research studies of the *Tourist Court Journal* reveal that motels on the average spend about 3.5 per cent of gross sales on advertising. American plan resorts spend about the same average percentage, but individual resorts in one study ranged from 1.2 per cent to 8.1 per cent.

All forms of advertising and sales promotion should be included in the budget. These consist of paid advertising, advertising fees, franchise fees, cost of endorsing and referral organizations, tourist association fees, outdoor signs, and other similar expenditures.

Commissions, discounts and allowances, such as those paid to authorized travel agents for business obtained, should not be included. Also, discounts on credit cards should not be considered as advertising. The foregoing recommendations are in accordance with the *Uniform Classification of Accounts for Motels and Motor Hotels.*

ADVERTISING MEDIA

There are at least two dozen media which could be employed. You will probably use less than half of this number. In planning your program, list the media considered as *essential, valuable,* and *probably helpful.* Your selection depends upon budget, goals, markets being sought and season of the year.

Importance of Timing

Your advertising program should be planned as far in advance as feasible. In the case of color cards or photographs to be used in printed advertising, a year in advance is necessary.

In your plan, list each month and then the advertising program which will be conducted monthly. Some programs such as signs, for example, would be in effect every month. Others would be seasonal, such as Christmas cards or notices of good fishing, color tours or skiing. Local events like homecoming, shows, ball games, bowling, tournaments, festivals, mushroom hunts, and similar events warrant various forms of advertising and precise timing.

If you are in a resort area, time your direct mail advertising with the period in the year when vacation plans are being made, usually in early spring. Having such a time schedule for advertising will help greatly to improve its effectiveness.

Word-of-Mouth Personal Advertising

This is the best, cheapest, and most convincing form of personal promotion. By being a friendly, interested, and capable host, you can quickly encourage this type of personal advertising. Treat every guest as a *Very Important Person* and he will not only come back himself but will recommend your place to his friends. All of your facilities, services, hospitality and pricing policies must be directed to this one goal—a satisfied, happy guest.

Outdoor Display Advertising

This medium is probably the most important single promotion method for motels. Signs must be carefully planned, located, and maintained to be effective. Impressions made by signs can do much to encourage (or discourage) patronage.

Between 85 and 90 per cent of all travelers go by automobile. As the traveler moves down the highway, his eye is attracted to a large number of advertising and directional signs. Because there are so many signs, an outdoor advertising program must be very skillfully planned and carried out to bring results. Leave this to the experts—outdoor advertising companies. These companies have found, for example, that related sales messages displayed close together impart a *concentrated impact.* The best procedure therefore is a planned system of signs carefully placed along the main highways leading to your business.

The most important single aspect of your sign system is *clever creative design.* Signs should be keyed to the architectural design of the building and incorporate a distinctive symbol. This symbol is effective in creating an impression on the prospect's mind. Signs can be interesting to read, which helps relieve the monotony of driving. You thus can provide outstanding signs which are designed and placed that they are welcomed by the traveler. When these creative, interesting and attractive signs are carefully placed and well maintained, it means the difference between successful sign advertising and just some signs.

Signs can do the following:
- —Identify you
- —Create an impression
- —Give directions
- —Sell meeting facilities
- —Sell entertainment
- —Help make decisions

Thus, they help to increase profits. In signs, emphasize what you have that your competitors do not. This establishes "differentiation."

"Feeder signs" are signs remote from your location, leading the prospect to you. These should be placed in open areas not cluttered by other signs. They will then receive the most attention. (Note: be careful to observe zoning or other restrictions on signs.)

The most important highway advertising appears just before reaching your business. This location justifies large displays to identify the business and give directions.

In areas where new superhighways have cut motels off from the previous main highway, cooperative signs (perhaps as large as 30' by 80') are very helpful.

Outdoor displays should be lighted or incorporate reflective materials. Over 40 per cent of all travel is done after dark and 66 per cent of all motel guests arrive after dark.[1]

Signs should always be maintained in tip-top condition.

Newspaper Advertising

Newspapers are helpful in promoting business for motels, particularly for food and beverage sales.

Transient motels and resorts are probably best served by ads in special travel issues. These special travel sections highlight the periods of volume tourist and vacation sales. Moreover, they direct the readers to specific vacation areas. Thus, you could support a tourist association advertising effort which boosts your area as well as a specific ad for your own business.

By doing market analysis as previously described, you can discover where your present business originates. This information will suggest possibilities for newspaper advertising.

Motels in resort areas can sometimes make more of an impression if they cooperate in a group advertisement sponsored by the Chamber of Commerce or tourist association. The newspaper will provide an attractive heading which features your resort area.

Magazine Advertising

Recent market research in regard to the magazine market indicates that heads of households who read magazines regularly do 28 per cent more pleasure traveling during the year than the heads of households regularly exposed to the other major national media. In addition, they did 32 per cent more miles of pleasure travel the past year than the

---

[1]According to Mr. Walter S. Meyers, General Manager, National Advertising Company.

U.S. average.[2] A ready market therefore exists which can be reached through magazine advertising. Your advertising agency can help to select the most likely magazines and the time of year the ads should be placed.

Ads in sportsmen's magazines should bring excellent results for motels in good hunting and fishing areas. Other possibilities would be brides' magazines for honeymoon business or travel magazines read by those who are interested in stimulating or unusual vacation suggestions.

Tourist Association Guide Books and Literature

These publications are attractive and substantial, providing important media for carrying motel and resort advertising.

Distribution of the guides is made primarily in response to direct inquiry and request for them. Thus, they are pinpointed directly to the individual who is seeking vacation suggestions. Contact your tourist promotion association representative for information.

Printed Literature

The average person is exposed to some 6,000 advertising impressions per day from signs, posters, newspapers, magazines, radio, TV, and other media. He has so many forces trying to persuade him to buy that any printed advertising must be done right and be effectively distributed to be worth its cost.

Here are some basic rules of printed advertising which should be followed:

a. *Get to the point.* Don't beat around the bush. Be brief and to the point. Often your second paragraph will be a better beginning than an introductory one which you first write.

b. *Give the information that people want.* If you were planning to stay at an unfamiliar motel, what would you wish to know about the place? Your answers to this question will help outline the information needed in your folder. Quote prices, how to get there, clothes to wear at the place, entertainment features, and similar information.

c. *Be different, if possible.* One of the keys to successful advertising is to be distinctive—outstanding—or different. Attract attention and induce the prospect to buy. This is done by creative thinking

---

[2]Duncan Miller, "Profitable Difference in Magazine Advertising," *Resort Management*, December, 1960, pp. 24-25.

and ideas which are novel and develop interest in the motel or resort.

Post Cards

Full color cards are indeed a handy and inexpensive advertising medium for any type of motel business. They are very helpful in writing short messages and can even carry a printed reservation acknowledgment. Several cards may be desirable, showing various exterior and interior views.

When composing a card, avoid showing large areas of sky. It is better to divide the card so that a portion shows the sign, perhaps an exterior close up view, or an interior view. The extra large cards do not mail well. A larger card with standard width (3 1/2" x 8 1/4") is very attractive, however, and is especially suitable for motels. *Use your identification symbol* on the cards as well as on your stationery, matches, business cards, and signs.

Giving cards to your guests will encourage them to mail them to relatives and friends. Use the card as part of your direct mail solicitation. If you have only a few forms of printed advertising, the color card should be one of your most essential pieces of literature.

Other types of cards are also useful. These include Christmas cards for guests with whom you have become well acquainted, birthday cards, anniversary cards, and reminder cards sent about a week or 10 days prior to the guest's arrival.

Folders or Brochures

Folders or brochures constitute one of the most effective forms of printed advertising. Nothing so completely tells the story of your place as does the folder. All types of motel businesses can use folders. The most convincing of all features well-chosen full color photographs of the principal attractions of the place. Art work is also commonly used, particularly when buildings and rooms are not involved.

Good folders include a rate sheet (which is printed separately), a reservation form, examples of activities, map and description location. Of course, there are variations in presentation. The map and other components could be printed separately.

Additional information should be provided as follows: address; phone number (including the "area code" to facilitate direct distance dialing); services provided; eating facilities; food specialties; plane, train and bus connections, and car rental services. The primary recreational attractions should be included such as golf, swimming, trails, sightseeing, and similar recreational advantages.

A professionally designed folder is money well spent. The same applies to the use of a professional photographer. Better to have no folder than a poor one.

By all means include printed descriptions of your nearby area. Prospective guests are more likely to come if you tell them about the many interesting and enjoyable points of interest they can enjoy in your vicinity.

STATIONERY

Most business stationery commonly lacks imagination and "punch." It should be colorful, interesting—yet dignified. Using the same color scheme as the exterior of the motel and also a symbol, if possible, helps to make stationery distinctive and eye-catching. Art work or a photograph also adds interest. The envelopes should be just as interesting as the writing paper and give the reader a "lift" and lasting impression of the motel or resort.

Direct Mail

At present, experience seems to indicate that direct mail has been more successful in the resort business than in motels. Perhaps the explanation lies in the greater experience of resorts with this medium.

Direct mail advertising has the advantage of preselection of prospects. Your advertising message goes directly to that person, privately and personally. Its value depends on several important factors:

1. The quality and impact of the mailing piece.
2. The validity of the prospect's interest in what you have to offer.
3. The frequency of mailing.

1. QUALITY AND IMPACT OF THE MAILING PIECE

Assuming that you have produced printed literature which is really good, the next step is to use this literature for direct mailing. A personal letter is best if you can spare the time to write. The next best thing is a reproduced letter which is individually addressed and personally signed. A personal postscript in your own handwriting is very good also. When making a mailing to a first-time prospect, send *complete* information so that the prospect's questions are completely answered. He should not have to write for additional information. This is particularly true regarding *rates*. Provide full, easily understood rate schedules. Then a follow-up letter in a week or so could be sent to show a continuing interest in the prospect's business.

If *you* were a prospective guest, what would *you want to know* about your place? Think this through and then organize your direct mailing pieces accordingly. Literature should tend to understate rather than overstate. Then when guests arrive they can say "This is lovelier than I thought."

Publicity associated with a magazine or newspaper article can be used advantageously for direct mail. People tend to be skeptical of advertising literature. But when they can read an article by a travel authority, they are likely to be impressed and to want to enjoy the place themselves.

If you can accommodate family trade, go after it. The children grow up quickly and soon become prospective customers themselves. As a matter of fact, catering to women guests and children is very smart business because they usually have the most to say about where the family will vacation each year. If the kids had a wonderful time at "Whispering Pines Inn," chances are they will be very anxious to return there again.

In your advertising, feature advantages and activities that women and children like and appreciate. For example, some motels have special equipment and recreation programs for children. A successful Michigan motel features a convenient laundry service, which is particularly appreciated by mothers. At vacation's end, the family can return home with their extra clothing all clean and freshly laundered.

2.   VALIDITY OF PROSPECT'S INTEREST

Mailing lists can be obtained from many different sources.

Foremost among these are your previous guests. Be sure that names and addresses are correct on registration cards. Then keep these lists in ready-to-use form, like addressing plates or on cards. Multiple-typed address stickers look rather cheap and are not easily read on the third or fourth copy. It is better to address each letter individually than to use this method.

Inquiry lists of the tourist promotion associations provide another good source of prospects. The type of vacation is shown on the inquiry list and this is a real help.

Inquiries received by chambers of commerce and convention bureaus are other sources of names.

Purchased lists from various sources. Lists can be obtained concerning almost every type of prospect. For example, you can get lists of sportsmen, people in various income brackets, retired couples, housewives and many others.

For lists of individuals as well as other types of lists, write the R. L. Polk Company, 431 Howard Street, Detroit, Michigan. Concerning associations, a good source is Encyclopedia of American Associations published by Gale Research Company, Book Tower Building, Detroit 26, Michigan.

Other sources of names. There are a few other ways to get names of prospects. Here are some ideas: those who have written you, but never made reservations, suggestions from your regular commercial guests and other guests, and from your employees. These may provide some excellent prospects.

Mailing Suggestions

When answering inquiries, be sure to send your material immediately. Answer all mail the same day, if possible. Send your folder, post card, a personal letter, and if feasible, a piece of cedar, birch bark, or similar object which may be symbolic of your place.

An area folder describing the wide advantages of your location is also a most compelling sales piece. Most vacationers are interested in the attractions beyond the bounds of your own property. They like side trips to points of interest such as summer, theaters, art works, historical sites, scenic drives, places for picnics, and other attractions.

Motels can do effective direct mail advertising, particularly for special events such as a bowling tournament or similar activity. However, long distance phone calls (as well as local calls) can be more valuable than direct mail in many instances. You can select your prospects by phone and do a considerable amount of business in this manner.

3. FREQUENCY OF MAILINGS

Seldom does a one-mailing campaign produce satisfactory results. Make several mailings but the minimum should be once a year to all previous guests. (For special events, one mailing may be sufficient, but this is an exception.) Seasonal mailings at times when prospective guests are planning trips are recommended. Some managers mail once a month. Probably a seasonal mailing of three or four times per year is best. Advice from a direct mail specialist, public relations or advertising agency, and from experienced managers is of most value.

Radio

For transient business, radio is important among advertising media as studies show that the majority of motorists do not make advance reservations. Spot announcements on the radio can reach the prospect and influence his decision. From 88 to 90 per cent of all cars have radios.

SELECTION OF A STATION

If prospective guests are coming to your place from large cities, then a powerful station covering that city is the best station to use. Smaller stations are effective in more sparsely settled areas. A large coverage is best because it provides a radio signal for a long time as the driver moves rapidly towards his destination.

A directory of all U.S. radio stations can be obtained from *Broadcasting-Telecasting*, 1735 De Sales St., Washington, D. C. Also, your local radio station can help you locate stations which might be effective. Compare for audience rating as well as power.

TIMING

1. Go for power—the wider the area covered, the better. The longer the driver hears the station, the more likely he will get the message and be influenced. Afternoon and early evening spot announcements are recommended.

2. For resort motels, use spot announcements on radio during the day. The morning is advantageous as this period is beamed to reach the women, who often make the decisions regarding the choice of vacation accommodations. Radio listening is now greater in summer than in winter. This is a reversal of listening patterns of the past and has been brought about the popularity of transistor radios.

3. Give radio a fair trial before making a decision regarding its effectiveness. Radio advertising people suggest using it for about three months before evaluation. Ask your guests how they heard about your place and tabulate their answers. Then you can see how radio fared as an advertising medium.

Television

Managers of resorts and motels have learned that television is too costly for the individual businessman. In a community with a rather large number of resorts and motels, however, group TV advertising sponsored by the chamber of commerce or a tourist association would be feasible. This should help attract businesses to your area and each individual business would then get its share of the trade.

Miscellaneous and Gimmick Advertising Media

There are many other advertising media which may have a place in the advertising program.

Maps

Litterbags

Shoeshine cloths

Bath mats

Business cards

Blotters

Key chains

Swimming suit bags or wrappers

Powdered detergent for hand
 laundering

Book matches (the regular size
 is best)

Shower caps and shoes

Rain hats for women

Ash tray souvenirs

Pencils, pens, pen desk sets

Pocket folders and notebooks

Decorated souvenir tumblers

Guest pac

Café pac

Souvenirs of local interest

Courtesy cards

Christmas cards

Calendars (including a 4-year
 version)

Yellow pages of the telephone
 book

Bumper strips

Matches

Pencils

City map guides

Hoisery mending kits

Mileage memo books

Outdoor thermometers

Plastic stir-forks

Knives (small)

Sewing kits

Lipettes folders

Emery board folders

Eye glasses cleaner

Snapshots of guests

Comments. The courtesy card is simply a card having a space in which the person's name is typed or written and bearing a statement that full courtesies should be shown this individual. This card is the correct size to fit in a person's wallet or purse and provides a handy reminder of the name, telephone number and address of the motel.

Christmas cards can be sent to those with whom you have become well acquainted. These cards provide a fine opportunity to express appreciation and send greetings.

A word of warning concerning the use of these forms of advertising. There is no sure-fire formula for their success. You will have to experiment before finding the best combination of all possible media—that combination in which all parts supplement and complement each other to produce maximum results.

REFERRAL AND ENDORSING ASSOCIATIONS

Referral Organizations

A referral organization's primary purpose is to increase sales. All members strive to refer business to other motels in the association by inviting guests to make reservations for their next night's stay.

Each motel member displays a distinctive membership sign which tells the prospective guest that this particular motel has met all requirements for membership. These requirements are generally recognized as high standards for the industry. Directories or guides are published in the millions by these organizations.

Membership in a referral association is often advisable. Many travelers hesitate to patronize a motel which is not a member of a referral or endorsing organization. The costs are deductible as advertising expense and if a record is kept of the business which is generated by such a membership, a factual evaluation of its effectiveness can be made.

Examples of such organizations are Best Western Motels, Congress Motels, Master Hosts, Quality Courts Motels Inc. and Superior Motels, Inc.

Endorsing Associations

Promotion of business through *inspection* and *approval* is the primary purpose of endorsing associations. They provide a prominent sign for display. The sign is normally the property of the endorsing association. In this way, they control issue and return of the signs.

Referral organizations are also endorsing associations, as they inspect and approve all of the members. The endorsing associations are primarily approval groups, however, certifying to the prospective guest that the establishment meets their standards and is operated in a manner conducive to the comfort, safety, convenience and satisfaction of the guests. Guides are also published in huge quantities by these groups.

Examples of endorsing associations are American Automobile Association, American Travel Association, Inc., and Dominion Automobile Association.

CHAMBERS OF COMMERCE

Many community or area chambers of commerce do an outstanding job of tourist promotion and travel information service. Tourists frequently contact the chamber of commerce in areas which hold vacation interest. Many chambers have attractive and well located information offices which provide referrals to member motels.

These chambers can thus be most helpful and an important source of your business. Your membership helps to get travelers into your community and into your place of business.

TRAVEL AGENCIES

How Travel Agents Function

Authorized travel agents number approximately 2,500 in the United States and abroad. These agents procure business for motels and resorts just as they do for airlines, steamships, and railroads. Business directly traced to a travel agent requires a 10 per cent commission. There also are associated benefits to travel agency business such as word-of-mouth advertising and personal referrals which can be very valuable.

Many accommodations businesses could well use travel agency business, particularly in the off season. Such business can be stimulated by a joint sales venture with travel agents. Any business generated is mutually beneficial to both the travel agency and the motel.

At the present time, travel agents feel that the initiative should be taken by the motel manager. He should assemble all available information concerning his motel and send or take it to the travel agent (or agents) deemed most likely to develop business for him.

The motel manager must keep the travel agent *fully* informed. In order to get and keep satisfied customers, the travel agency must have up-to-date information on rates, dates of opening and closing, latest pictures and literature and anything else helpful to the travel agent in selling a person on the particular location. Any special weekend tours or package rates should be promptly supplied to the agent.

Business Potential Through Travel Agents

If you have obtained a market analysis, as described in this book, you will have reached some conclusions concerning good sources of business.

For example, if you get considerable patronage out of Detroit and Toledo, then working with some successful travel agents in these cities might be very fruitful. The same would apply to Chicago or any of the cities—large and small—from which you draw trade.

To help you locate travel agents, the American Society of Travel Agents, 501 Fifth Avenue, New York 17, New York, has published a directory of agents in each state and abroad. This directory entitled *Your Hotel's Most Powerful Sales Team* also includes the "Agency-Hotel Fair Play Code" formulated to smooth relations between these segments of the travel industry. A copy of this directory can be obtained by writing to the society at the address given.

MOTEL BUSINESS AND TRADE ASSOCIATIONS

Motel trade associations exist to: 1) assist in getting favorable legislation passed and in defeating unfavorable legislation; 2) assist in educating members to run better motels and more profitable businesses; 3) advertise and promote an area so that motels within that area do a better business.

Trade associations available to motels are: The American Motor Hotel Association, the American Hotel and Motel Association, and the National Restaurant Association, if food service is provided. The state motel associations are affiliated with the American Motor Hotel Association.

Dues in the state associations are usually graduated according to the size of the business. Membership in the state association brings automatic membership in both the national association and the local chapters.

INTERNAL SELLING AND ADVERTISING

Selling outside of the business is usually thought to be the sole concern of the sales effort. However, internal selling—all sales efforts made after guests have been registerd—can and should be an important part of the advertising program. Internal selling has two purposes, namely to encourage the guest to patronize all facilities of your business and to influence him favorably to return again.

Personal Selling

Inasmuch as the most impelling type of selling is personal selling, this aspect of internal selling provides an excellent potential for increasing business. All of your staff should be sales-minded. They need training to immediately recognize the ever-present need for offering a sales suggestion to a guest when the opportunity presents itself.

Here are some examples:

Manager while registering a guest: "Mr. Brown, we have a beautiful new dining room here and hope that you can try it out. We're also open for breakfast, beginning at 7:00 A.M."

Manager while rooming a guest: (in hot weather) "If you'd care for a mint julep before dinner, you can have one in the cocktail lounge."

Waitress serving dinner: "We feature warm Michigan cherry pie. Would you like some for dessert?"

Other Methods[3]

Internal selling can be done by means of various printed pieces or by article posters and similar methods. Examples are:

Tent cards	Morning paper with sticker
Posters	Menus
Lighted pictures of guest rooms, dining, and beverage rooms	Cocktail napkins
	Bulletin boards
Ads under dresser top (glass)	Elevator cards
Reminder cards	Stiff paper folder containing ads
Bathroom mirror stickers	

CONVENTION AND GROUP BUSINESS

Excellent Potential

Many motels and resort motels could do more group business with their present facilities. Others could develop this type of patronage with some remodeling or enlarging.

There is a considerable demand for good meeting places for small groups—10 to 40 persons or so. These may be representatives of a small company, sales, engineering, executive, or similar groups who need a quiet place to conduct their affairs. Many motels and resorts appeal to these groups due to their location in small communities or in isolated places, free from the competition of theaters, places to shop, and night spots.

There is no definite line between getting convention business and keeping it. Word-of-mouth is the best method of selling. Good location, pleasant site, friendly atmosphere and delicious food are all important in selling your service. Satisfied guests will do most of your selling. Treat every guest as a V.I.P. and he will lead you to group business. Regardless of how guests look when they come into your establishment, treat them as V.I.P.'s. Be enthusiastic. It's catching and helps sell your place.

Today, more than any time before, you must have recreational advantages to draw conventions and group business. These include such activities as bowling, good fishing sites, and swimming.

---

[3]For additional guidance on advertising, see *How to Make Advertising Pay for Hotels, Motels, and Restaurants* by Albert E. Koehl, published by Ahrens Publishing Co.

Transportation to your place is also very important—air transportation, train and bus schedules.

Prospective guests want to know the type of plan you have, American or European. It would be good to have both plans and a variety within each plan. Have package plans including bowling, golf, or boating, or other recreation if possible.

Selling Conventions and Group Business

Initially, management must view the sales problem in convention business *as a problem-solving service* for the organization being solicited. *You are not selling your facilities for the group—you are selling the ability of your resort or motel to solve their meeting problems.*

The sales person mentally solves the prospect's problems (through his meeting facilities) before actually mentioning these facilities. Only when he has completed this mental process does he describe the many advantages of his place. The sales person will have little problem selling what he has to offer when he approaches the prospect in this manner.

On an even higher plane of sales strategy and service is the employment of motel or resort *sales representatives who are capable of assisting the convention chairman to promote and conduct the convention.* The sales representative thus acts as a consultant on meetings, suggests an agenda, names of speakers, conduct of various parts of the convention, how to promote attendance, and similar matters.

Making your motel the adult education center of the community is another possibility. Your sales director can become proficient in arranging and coordinating adult educational meetings and conferences held at the motel. An excellent potential exists for this type of meeting facility and the demand is growing. People are more educationally minded now than ever before.

Aids in Selling

1. An attractive sales display kit is essential in selling group business. This kit is of loose-leaf construction containing large plastic envelopes for displaying every bit of information needed by a group chairman. Needless to say, the sales person must be thoroughly familiar with all conceivable aspects of the accommodation.

The kits should include diagrams of meeting rooms, pictures, lists of services, recreational advantages, games, menus and various dining arrangements, and similar descriptions.

2. A brochure should be given to the prospect, to be placed in his files for future reference.

3. A complimentary luncheon should be offered to the prospect, or if he represents a large group, perhaps a weekend at the place would be in order. This experience will thoroughly acquaint him with the facility so he can better visualize holding his meeting there.

4. Complete and vigorous follow-up of sales contacts or inquiries is advisable. If a reply is not soon received to the first letter, a phone call is recommended and then another letter which confirms what was said on the phone. This is good business. It impresses the prospect with your business-like methods and enthusiasm for what you have to offer.

5. Reminders concerning conventions are usually needed. About 90 per cent of those who plan conventions don't know exactly what they want. You have to sell your facilities as a place where their *meeting problems can be solved.*

Keep in mind the group's need for:

—Registration desk	—Slide projectors
—Ticket collection	—P.A. system
—Photographers	—Lighting
—Blackboards	—Exhibits
—Easels	—Favors
—Lecterns	—Cards
—Motion picture machines	—Cigarettes

Motel Group Business in Urban Locations

For motels in urban centers, good results can be accomplished in selling them for local meetings and food business. Consider the following suggestions:

1. Conduct an organized and well planned sales campaign.

2. Create an effective sales display kit.

3. Have a very attractive printed brochure which can be left with the prospect for his file.

4. Select prospects from among local:
   a. Businesses and offices
   b. Stores
   c. Factories
   d. Organizations such as clubs and fraternal organizations
   e. Association representatives
   f. Sales offices of large concerns

In short, look for prospects in any business or social organization which might have need for your meeting rooms, guest rooms, food services, party facilities or any other function which your motel can fulfill.

5. For your "sales blitz" hire bright local boys (or possibly young women). College students are a possibility if located nearby. They must be able to provide full answers to questions.

6. Actual selling is confined to telling the high-ranking officers or managers of each firm about the advantages of holding meetings or other functions in your motel, using the problem-solving technique previously described.

7. A follow-up letter in two or three days shows a continuing interest in the prospect's account.

8. The blitz should be repeated about three times each year, calling on those who have not responded to the sales efforts.

The effects of this effort will probably not be immediate, but within a month or so there should be a very satisfactory response.

EVALUATING YOUR PROMOTION PROGRAM

The only satisfactory way in which an advertising and sales promotion program can be factually evaluated is to ask the guest how he happened to select your place.

Some methods are easy to determine, such as referrals or replies from newspaper advertisements. For the remainder, however, you will need to devise a special method for getting the essential information. A courteous inquiry such as "Mr. Brown, how did you happen to choose our place?" is the recommended way to learn about the advertising media which is doing the job.

CHAPTER 21

Proficiency
in Management

No business consistently stands still. It either goes up or goes down. These are changing times, and every business must constantly be aware of trends and be ready to meet whatever challenge comes along. This is the responsibility of management.

More and more, motel owners are recognizing the importance of hiring qualified managers—not just anyone who happens to be out of work or professes great interest in the occupation. But how does one become "qualified"? Few existing motel managers are now successful who do not possess technical *knowledge, skill,* and love for their service role.

Adequate skill comes through experience. Even the finest educational program has difficulty in teaching the skill of operating a motel. Anyone hoping to enter the field of motel management as a full-time occupation should first gain experience by working in some capacity in a well-established motel operation. He thus can observe how day-to-day and long range decisions are made and the many, many problems requiring action by a manager. There is no substitute for experience.

Few managers succeed very long if they do not believe in their occupation. All the skill or knowledge in the world will not adequately equip a manager to face the day-by-day challenge of serving the traveling public. The public is whimsical, capricious, and ever-changing. Unless you can love this work, it is not for you. Contrary to popular opinion, the money rewards are not great and satisfaction must come from other sources.

Adequate knowledge is becoming more and more important as the occupation and facilities become more complex. Both the inexperienced and the established manager need all the knowledge they can acquire.

For the young person electing motel management as a career, the best way of obtaining adequate knowledge is at the colleges or universities offering degrees in hotel and motel management. We are fortunate in the United States to have several institutions with long tenure in this type of educational emphasis. At these schools the individual receives instruction in this specialized phase of management as well as the broadening background of a college education. Those who have had this formal training generally find that they progress more rapidly and receive greater employment opportunities than those without it.

For the person now in business, several opportunities for self-improvement are available today. For example, one of the ways to become a better manager is to carefully read every pertinent article in the trade magazines. Much excellent material appears in these publications which can help an individual become a more expert manager.

Many state motel associations are sponsoring short courses or institutes in cooperation with their state college or university. Specialists in a variety of subject matter can describe the application of their fields to the motel business. For example, an advertising professor can explain some principles of advertising and then the group can study how these principles can best be applied to the motel industry. Similar subjects include business management, psychology, food service, personnel management and other important subjects. Attendance at these schools helps to develop a keener insight into management problems and their suggested solutions. Announcements concerning these schools are regularly found in the trade journals.

Annual conventions of the state and national trade associations are educational, cultural, and entertaining. This is also true of the annual meetings of referral organizations.

Home study materials in the form of bulletins, circulars, and folders are published by the cooperative extension service of every state land grant college and university. These publications include numerous subjects of interest to motel managers. Examples are those on lawn care, flowers and shrubs, interior decoration, insect control and food service. For a list of available publications, write to your Cooperative Extension Service. A complete list of offices appears in the Annotated Bibliography which follows.

The Educational Institute of the American Hotel and Motel Association provides opportunity for home-study as well as group-study of hotel and motor hotel management subjects. These include *Your Hotel and Its Economy* (an introductory course), *Front Office Management, Accounting, Engineering,* and similar courses. Information is available by writing to their office, Kellogg Center, Michigan State University, East Lansing.

A library of books is also very useful. Several outstanding books have been prepared to aid the motel manager. An excellent bibliography is published by the School of Hotel Administration, Cornell University, Ithaca, New York. The bibliography is published annually and should be on the bookshelf of every motel manager.

Get-togethers in your local motel association are almost always productive of some good ideas. The exchange of information obtained from experience and practice is mutually helpful.

A new program of recognition for those who strive to achieve a high degree of managerial perfection has been suggested by J. Pendleton Gaines, executive vice-president of the Florida Motel Association. The program has been designated as "Certified Public Host" or C.P.H. A certificate of recognition would be awarded to each motel manager who has met certain requirements of professional improvement. Widespread adoption of this program of recognition would be of great value in upgrading and bringing even more prestige to the occupation of motel keeping.

A concluding photographic essay of a motel which exemplifies the basic precepts of this book. The Snow Flake Motel of St. Joseph, Michigan has a *location* most favorable for high occupancy today: within a few minutes drive of many "generators of trade." It has outstanding *facilities*, expressing the ultimate in modern comfort and architectural appeal. Finally, it has superior operational *management*, which brings about the highly coveted goal of all motel entrepreneurs: high occupancy resulting from guest satisfaction.

The Snow Flake Motel was designed by architect William Wesley Peters of Taliesin Associated Architects, an affiliate of the Frank Lloyd Wright Foundation. It is owned and managed by Mr. Sahag Sarkisian.

This bird's-eye view of the Snow Flake Motel illustrates how the design motif is expressed in the site arrangement of the building. It does not appear forced and binds the entire facility with its singular theme.

A. This sparkling design as seen from the roadside is a refreshing change from the normally blocky massiveness of most motels.

B. An airy enclosure of steel serves as a visual link among the swimming pool, restaurant, cocktail lounge and conference room.

C. The snowflake motif is expertly adapted to the warmth of the landscape setting in summer. The unusual facade avoids the common and monotonous "boxcar" motel architecture.

D. The light feathery motif of the snowflake is well expressed in this illuminated entrance sign.

E. In a region where sunshine is at a premium, maximum light is allowed through the open roof structure. Notice the hexagonal shadow pattern on the walk.

The snow crystal design which is the symbol for the building architecture, the entrance sign, and promotional literature for the motel. Such a symbol of the theme makes a lasting impression upon all who view it.

Annotated Bibliography

ANNOTATED BIBLIOGRAPHY

A B C of Supervision. Urbana: University of Illinois Bulletin, Bureau of Business Management No. 601, 1958.

The elements of supervising employees in order to achieve a happy, effective staff.

HECKMAN, I. L. JR., AND HUNERYAGER, S.G. *Human Relations in Management.* Cincinnati: South-Western Publishing Co., 1960.

A textbook which provides a unique blending of text material and selected articles written by authorities in the human relations field. Basic concepts and principles concerning people at work are emphasized.

JOSEPHSON, MATTHEW. *Union House, Union Bar.* New York: Random House, 1956.

The history of the hotel and restaurant employees and bartenders international union, AFL-CIO.

LEAVITT, HAROLD J. *Managerial Psychology.* Chicago: The University of Chicago Press, 1958.

A book which clearly outlines methods of solving problems associated with supervising and managing personnel.

LUNDBERG, DONALD E. *Personnel Management in Hotels and Restaurants.* Dubuque, Iowa: William C. Brown Co., 1955.

A very complete and well written compilation of personnel management principles found to be helpful in hotels, motels and restaurants. Describes the Harris, Kerr, Forster Payroll Cost Control System, increasing employees' satisfaction through sound promotion policies, job titles, pay incentives, profit-sharing, bonus plans and many, many other important aspects of personnel management.

PETERSON, ROBERT L. *Work Incentives for your Personnel.* Urbana: University of Illinois Bulletin, Bureau of Business Management Bulletin No. 503, 1955.

A most helpful and clearly written description of the use of work incentives for small business organizations.

PIGAGE, L. C., AND TUCKER, J. L. *Job Evaluation.* Urbana: University of Illinois Bulletin Volume 5, No. 3, 1959.

A detailed booklet which describes the methods of establishing job evaluations for each position in your business.

SIBSON, ROBERT E. *Wages and Salaries:* A handbook for Line Managers. New York: American Management Association, Inc., 1960.

This handbook gives the manager necessary information about wage and salary techniques and basic data on job evaluation, merit rating, wage incentives, fringe benefits, and compensation for exempt and non-exempt employees.

THE STORY OF PROFIT SHARING and what it may mean to you. Chicago: Council of Profit Sharing Industries.

This booklet, endorsed by the National Restaurant Association, gives the history of the development of profit sharing, how it works, and what is necessary to start a plan of your own.

THERE'S ALWAYS A BETTER WAY. Midland, Michigan: The Dow Chemical Company.

Here is a most interesting and understandable description of how to bring the advantages of work simplification to your business. Illustrated with amusing cartoons.

GIEDION, S. *Space, Time and Architecture.* Cambridge: Harvard University Press, Third Edition, 1959.

A professional work, to be read by those seriously seeking answers to the apparent confusion in architecture and how it relates to modern living.

RASKIN, EUGENE. *Architecturally Speaking.* New York, Reinhold Publishing Corp., 1954.

This is a must for all who seek a fresh, easy-to-read, but provocative review of the traditional elements of architectural design.

Moser, C. A. *Survey Methods in Social Investigation*. New York, Macmillan Co., 1958.

A complete but brief summary of modern surveys: what they can and cannot reveal; how to make them; and what they can mean.

Editors of Architectural Forum. *Building, U. S. A.*

A critical review of the many influences (in addition to architects) in today's design of buildings.

Architectural Record Book, *Hotels, Motels, Restaurants, and Bars*. New York: S. W. Dodge Corp., Second Edition, 1960.

A fine collection of actual cases, well illustrated, together with descriptive information on planning and construction.

Simonds, John Ormsbee. *Landscape Architecture*. New York: F. W. Dodge Corp., 1961.

A comprehensive philosophy and also practical guide on site planning and its significance in all structures today.

List of addresses of Cooperative Extension Offices:

Alabama	Auburn University, Auburn.
Alaska	Agricultural Experiment Station, Palmer.
Arizona	University of Arizona, Tucson.
Arkansas	University of Arkansas, Little Rock.
California	Extension Service, University of California, Berkeley.
Colorado	Colorado State University, Fort Collins
Connecticut	University of Connecticut, Storrs.
Delaware	University of Delaware, Newark.
Florida	Horticultural Building, University of Florida, Gainesville.
Georgia	College of Agriculture, University of Georgia, Athens.
Hawaii	University of Hawaii, Honolulu.
Idaho	317 1/2 North Eighth Street, Boise.
Illinois	College of Agriculture, University of Illinois, Urbana.
Indiana	Purdue University, Lafayette.
Iowa	Iowa State University, Ames.
Kansas	Kansas State University, Manhattan.
Kentucky	College of Agriculture, University of Kentucky, Lexington.
Louisiana	Louisiana State University, University Station, Baton Rouge.

Maine .... College of Agriculture, University of Maine, Orono.
Maryland .... University of Maryland, College Park.
Massachusetts ...... University of Massachusetts, Amherst.
Michigan .... Michigan State University, East Lansing.
Minnesota .... University of Minnesota, St. Paul.
Mississippi .... Mississippi State College, Starkville.
Missouri .... University of Missouri, Columbia.
Montana .... Montana State College, Bozeman.

Nebraska .... University of Nebraska, Lincoln.
Nevada .... University of Nevada, Reno.
New Hampshire .... University of New Hampshire, Durham.
New Jersey .... Rutgers—The State University, New Brunswick.
New Mexico .... New Mexico State University, University Park.
North Carolina ..... North Carolina State College, Raleigh.
New York .... New York State College, Ithaca.
North Dakota .... North Dakota State University, Fargo.

Ohio .... The Ohio State University, Columbus.
Oklahoma .... Oklahoma State University, Stillwater.
Oregon .... Oregon State University, Corvallis.

Pennsylvania .... The Pennsylvania State University, University Park.
Puerto Rico .... University of Puerto Rico, Rio Piedras.

Rhode Island .... University of Rhode Island, Kingston.

South Carolina ..... Clemson Agricultural College, Clemson.
South Dakota .... South Dakota State College, College Station, Brookings

Tennessee .... College of Agriculture, University of Tennessee, Knoxville.
Texas .... Texas A. and M. College System, College Station.
Utah .... Utah State University of Agriculture and Applied Science, Logan.

Vermont .... College of Agriculture, University of Vermont, Burlington.

Virginia .... Virginia Polytechnic Institute, Blacksburg.
Washington .... Washington State University, Pullman.
West Virginia .... College of Agriculture, West Virginia University, Morgantown.
Wisconsin .... College of Agriculture, University of Wisconsin, Madison.
Wyoming .... College of Agriculture, University of Wyoming, Laramie.

Index